IMAGES
*of Sport*

# FEATHERSTONE ROVERS
# RUGBY LEAGUE CLUB

On the front cover, the Rovers acknowledge the part played by their coach, Laurie Gant, in their first Challenge Cup triumph in 1967. John Newlove was part of the 1967 squad and played in the semi-final, although he missed out at Wembley. This photograph shows him celebrating as the skipper of the 1973 side, which again secured the trophy for Rovers.

IMAGES
*of Sport*

# FEATHERSTONE ROVERS
# RUGBY LEAGUE CLUB

*Compiled by*
Ron Bailey

TEMPUS

First published 2001
Reprinted 2005
Copyright © Ron Bailey, 2001

Tempus Publishing Limited
The Mill, Brimscombe Port,
Stroud, Gloucestershire, GL5 2QG

ISBN 0 7524 2295 2

Typesetting and origination by
Tempus Publishing Limited
Printed in Great Britain

Paul Newlove, the son of John Newlove, scored 122 tries in 150 appearances in five seasons with the club from 1988 to 1993. In 1993 he was transferred to Bradford Northern. Rovers had reluctantly transfer listed him at £750,000; Bradford offered £150,000 and the matter was then referred to the Rugby League Transfer Tribunal who fixed a record fee (by tribunal) of £245,000. Two years later, Newlove moved to St Helens from Bradford in a deal reckoned to be worth £500,000.

# Contents

# Acknowledgements

Most of the photographs are from my own and the club's collections – which have been built from many sources over the years, including the *Pontefract & Castleford Express*, *Yorkshire Post*, *Yorkshire Evening Post*, *Bradford Telegraph & Argus*, *Hull Daily Mail*, *Halifax Courier*, *Sunday Express*, *Daily Express*, *The Guardian*, *Daily Mirror*, *The Sun*, *Manchester Evening News*, *Rugby Leaguer*, Kelmsley & Thomson Newspapers, South Lancs & Cheshire Press Service, Sport & General Press Agency, Press Association, Central Press Photos and Jack Hicks, Eric Lorriman, Sig Kasatkia and Robert Nunn. I am indebted to all these sources, without whose help the story could not have been told. The exact origins of some photographs are unknown. If any copyright has been infringed, there has been no deliberate intent to do so.

I would also like to acknowledge my appreciation of the assistance given by Terry Jones, chief executive of Featherstone Rovers, Irvin Saxton, Donald Hunt, Stephen Parker, Laurie Gant, Tony Lumb and Frank Waude, together with Tempus Publishing, for their help, guidance and patience. Finally, the inevitable thanks to my wife Maureen, who, after a lifetime of supporting me in my Rovers cause, continues to encourage and type manuscripts so capably; and to our son Mark for his perceptive and analytical review – all essential ingredients to the finished product.

In 1983, Terry Hudson became the third Rovers captain to lift the Challenge Cup.

# Introduction

This is the story of Featherstone Rovers, one of the less fashionable clubs in senior rugby league. Yet it is only less fashionable because of its limited resources, which have meant a continual battle for survival. This has been, and probably always will be, the case. Featherstone has the smallest population of any rugby league town – indeed, at 14,000, there was a time when the ground capacity exceeded that figure. The counter attraction of the Wakefield and Castleford clubs within such a small area is also a factor, but each club remains independently proud of its own existence, as was shown when the proposed merger of the three clubs was mooted in 1995.

Despite this handicap, the club has not only survived, but has also written its own place in the annals of Rugby League history. Surmounting the darkest days of the 1930s and '40s, its success in the second half of the last century is inspirational. The club has a particular association with glorious achievements in the Challenge Cup competition – starting with the marvellous 1952 campaign and sustained through the 1960s, '70s and '80s. The club's league performances, particularly in the early 1960s and mid-'70s, with the pinnacle of the First Division Championship in 1977, confirmed its consistency and ability to compete with the best. While the success story is not persistent throughout their history, it is enough to inspire and preserve the hope and spirit.

Indeed, the spirit engendered within the club is the key to its success. Featherstone is a community club around which the town revolves. Until the late 1980s, the town was dominated by the mining industry and, for most of the club's existence, miners have been a part of the Rovers set-up as a major source of players and support. The mining industry may have waned, but the closeness of the community still helps mould the spirit which has been handed down among players, officials and supporters alike, and which will continue to thrive whilst the game is played at Featherstone.

This story chronicles the triumphs of a Cinderella club pitted against the odds. Yet having reached its eightieth anniversary, there are many who feel that there are currently even greater challenges to face – and from within the game itself. The advent of Super League and summer football were accepted, but what lies in the aftermath? After five years, Featherstone Rovers and the other clubs outside the elite group of twelve Super League clubs find themselves in a precarious and, in some ways, an isolated position. They are naturally worried about the state of the game. What interested me in my research was the number of players and supporters who, like myself, consider that the modern game has lost its edge. Undoubtedly, the players are fitter and stronger athletes, and consequently the game is faster. Yet it has become, in comparison, more stereotypical and predictable and many Rovers stars of the past do not watch it. Be that as it may, it is still a great game, and one must not forget that many of today's supporters have known nothing else.

Featherstone's concern can be related to the fact that it has always existed against a background of limited resources and constant financial problems. It has survived not only because of indigenous spirit and determination, but also because of its renowned ability to discover and nurture outstanding talent from its local junior sources. That talent bred the successful Rovers teams and also enriched the game when, inevitably, the club had to off-load some of its stars. Rovers supporters have over the years found this difficult to stomach, but the blunt truth is that the club has so often had to sell to survive. Sadly, that talent source is now less productive, and there is no doubt that a considerable gap has opened in the respective ability levels of Super League and First Division teams. The pride of the local player in donning the Featherstone jersey has been diluted by the lure of Super League riches, and the likelihood of 'saviour' transfers has lessened considerably. Attendances, as ever, remain a problem and hardly cover players' wages – although this is a situation that has not changed in eighty years. Sponsorship and marketing are now major factors, but, mirroring the concerns felt in other aspects of the game, the emphasis is too heavily weighted to the elite super twelve, and it seems to leave only crumbs for the rest.

Can the rest exist on crumbs? With the dilution of its junior resources, Featherstone face this uncertainty with a cornerstone of its existence to date weakened. I have no doubt that the spirit which has prevailed will continue, however, and this is important. The club now has one of the most compact grounds in the league, and whilst the ground capacity has had to be considerably reduced, its accommodation and other facilities are better than ever before. This at least fulfils part of the criteria for Super League and there is no reason why Rovers cannot, once again, improve their playing strength through its traditional junior source. The solid supporter base that has bolstered the club in the past still exists and – although smaller than it has been – is something upon which to build. The glory days of the past decades may be but memories, but they are the inspiration which together with the pride Featherstone has in its team, provide the platform for Featherstone Rovers to face the future. Featherstone has long since learned to cope with its own problems. It is now up to the powers that be to move positively into the future, embracing the needs of the Super League and First Division clubs so that the Featherstone story can continue.

Featherstone born and bred, it has been my pleasure to trace the story of our team. I have been privileged to be part of this history, but inevitably the story has been influenced, to a degree, by the availability of material sources. Despite extensive searches, I have been disappointed by the lack of material from the early years and the successful 1970s (with that decade's Challenge Cup and league triumphs). Nevertheless, I hope this has not weakened the storyline and that all supporters will enjoy this nostalgic journey. For the older supporters, there will be the rekindling of memories; for the younger generation, the chance to learn of a fascinating heritage. The emphasis on players will be covered in far greater depth in the second of the Tempus publications on Featherstone Rovers, featuring the club's 100 greatest players (scheduled for publication in 2002) and the trilogy of publications will be concluded (in 2003) with a book covering 50 of the club's classic matches.

Ron Bailey
August 2001

# Chapter One

# The 1920s

The club played its first senior game at Bradford on 27 August 1921, winning 17-3. The first home match, played against Hull on 3 September, was officially opened by Mr Whittaker, the chairman of the Yorkshire Committee. Ten victories were gained in the season, but the Rovers realised that it was a hard learning process. The club's main focus in the 1920s was obviously on consolidation – not only from a playing but also a financial point of view. It was stated by Mr Johnson at the 1921 Annual General Meeting that gates of 5,000 were required for the club to pay its way. In their first season, the average attendance was 3,470 and receipts £164. Sadly, despite some improvement in league positions, those averages were not to be surpassed in the rest of the decade, and even in 1927/28, when the team finished third, gate receipts only totalled £2,167 – an average of £120.

There were contributing factors. With the admission of Castleford to senior rugby league in 1926, the effect of having three major clubs, Wakefield, Castleford and Featherstone, in such close proximity and competition, was established. Although not such a permanent problem, the prevailing economic depression, culminating in the General Strike of 1926, caused its own difficulties for the club and the community. Indeed, at the time of the strike, Rovers agreed to allow striking miners to pay 6d admission instead of the normal 1s.

Nevertheless, what did become clear in that first decade of senior football was that league attendances were not high enough to keep the club afloat, and survival therefore hinged on successful runs in cup competitions (for which support would appear), the transfer of promising players to other clubs, and contributions from Supporters Clubs – characteristics which have carried through to the present day. Interestingly, in 1927 the Rovers played Barrow at home in the first round of the Challenge Cup, won 14-0 and attracted a 5,000 gate. The following week, for a league fixture with Barrow, the attendance was 2,000.

From a playing point of view, the Rovers excelled themselves in 1928 by reaching the top four play-offs so soon after obtaining professional status, but generally there was disappointment in the results of other seasons. However, the comment made by Mr J.W. Wood, chairman of the Northern Rugby League at the time of Featherstone's application for senior status, that 'it seems good footballers are indigenous to the soil of Featherstone' has always rung true and has been the backbone of Rovers' existence. In cup competitions, notice of intent of providing shocks and giant-killing acts was served in the epic Challenge Cup encounter with Wigan in 1923, when the Rovers narrowly lost 14-13. Off the field, progress was made in consolidating the facilities available at the ground with the provision of a new stand, dressing rooms and improvements to terracing. The local Miners Welfare Committee purchased the ground from Umpleby Trustees for £1,500 and then rented it to the club. The events of this decade were indicative of the will and enthusiasm of the Featherstone fraternity to ensure the success of their rugby league team.

League Positions

| | P | W | D | L | For | Agst | Pts | % | Posn |
|---|---|---|---|---|---|---|---|---|---|
| 1921/22 | 36 | 10 | 2 | 24 | 274 | 463 | 22 | 30.5 | 24(26) |
| 1922/23 | 34 | 17 | 1 | 16 | 413 | 533 | 35 | 51.4 | 12(27) |
| 1923/24 | 36 | 12 | 3 | 21 | 348 | 545 | 27 | 37.5 | 23(27) |
| 1924/25 | 34 | 15 | 0 | 19 | 322 | 362 | 30 | 44.1 | 17(27) |
| 1925/26 | 32 | 15 | 2 | 15 | 362 | 362 | 32 | 50.0 | 12(23) |
| 1926/27 | 38 | 21 | 1 | 16 | 504 | 369 | 43 | 56.3 | 11(29) |
| 1927/28 | 36 | 25 | 1 | 10 | 387 | 236 | 51 | 70.8 | 3(29) |
| 1928/29 | 38 | 10 | 4 | 24 | 277 | 451 | 24 | 31.5 | 26(29) |
| 1929/30 | 36 | 12 | 3 | 21 | 268 | 398 | 27 | 37.5 | 23(28) |

(-) denotes number of clubs in the league

Featherstone Rovers owes its existence to Mr George Johnson, who was instrumental in setting up the club as a junior side originally in 1902 and again in 1908 after it had folded in 1906. The outstanding success of the team from 1919 to 1921 (when eight cups were won with 1,700 points scored and only 300 against), showed the Rovers to be in a class of their own in junior circles. An application was therefore made for admission to the Northern Rugby League. On 7 June 1921, Mr Johnson presented the club's case at a meeting in Manchester, accompanied by Mr J.W. McTrusty (finance chairman) and Mr G. Brearley (secretary). The application was accepted unanimously and the Rovers attained senior status for the 1921/22 season. George Johnson continued at the helm as chairman and then president until 1937, when he retired through ill-health. He served the club for almost thirty-five years and, with his shrewd football brain and business-like attitude, was described as one of the great administrators in the game. His son, George Johnson Jnr, signed for Rovers in 1931. He scored a record 23 points (10 goals and 1 try) against Bradford two months later, played for a Rugby League XIII in France in 1935 and was transferred to Hunslet in December 1935.

In their opening game at Bradford, the Rovers secured their first points after exactly one minute, when Jimmy Williams coolly dropped a goal. They went on to win 17-3. The team was: Smith, J. Denton, Hirst, Reeves, S. Denton, Williams, Kirkham, Dooler, Barraclough, Jones, Clements, Hepworth, Haigh. The first captain was Norman Reeves.

Jimmy Williams scored the Rovers' first points in senior rugby league and, with 3 goals and a try, was the star of the opening win against Bradford. The brother of Bill Williams, he made 211 appearances for Featherstone, scoring 30 tries and 120 goals (330 points), mainly at half-back. His last game was, however, on the wing – ironically, against Bradford – in a home fixture on 24 April 1929. He was granted a joint testimonial that season with Arthur Haigh, both receiving £50.

## CLUB NOTES.

Alderman Sir William Forster Todd should have a special interest in the visit of Featherstone Rovers to Clarence-street this evening, for it was the popular president of the York Club who did everything he could and ultimately proposed the admission of Featherstone to the ranks of senior competition football. More than this, Sir William, who is always willing to extend a helping hand and practical sympathy to those not by any means so well placed as himself, has a special pride in the fortunes of the club, towards which he has ever shown that kindly feeling which has made his name a household word throughout the county of which he is a native, not only in the matter of sport, but also in every cause which has for its object the helping over the stile of those who are not able to get over entirely unaided. Yes, out Featherstone way, Sir William Forster Todd is as popular as he is in York, and Sir William has the happy knack of never forgetting those who at any time render him and his cause a service. He is not unmindful of the fact that many of the members of the York team have at one time and another been drawn from the colliery district of which Featherstone is the centre, and no one was more genuinely proud than he of the fact that when York visited the Colliers' ground early in the present season, we returned victorious by one point only. There were many who could be forgiven for thinking that the Minster men had been hard put to it; but not so our president, for he alone outside the actual players knew of the secret instruction that had been given that York were not by any means to win by a huge margin of points. The instruction was to the effect that we had to win but not handsomely; we had to lend colour to the fact that the Rovers of Featherstone were worthy of the confidence we had placed in them by advocating that they should be raised to first-class status; and this our players loyally did, but it has to be admitted that the line was very finely drawn, and the margin was so close that we should have been bested had the Rovers kicked their goal in the closing stages of the game; we were indeed fortunate to keep the Rovers out in the last few seconds of the match, for they were then clearly playing for victory and were easily the

Extract from a York programme in 1922. Do we believe they were so benevolent? York had already beaten Featherstone 7-6 and went on to win this return game at their own ground 18-10.

One of the first transfers was that of John William Higson from Huddersfield in September 1921. As a Featherstone junior, he had been signed by Hunslet in 1906, becoming part of the 'Terrible Six' pack which helped Hunslet win all four cups in 1907/08. Higson had moved to Huddersfield in their heyday, prior to the First World War, and won more medals than any other player in the game. At Featherstone he was appointed captain almost immediately, when Norman Reeves was ruled out through injury for the rest of the season. In 1925, Higson was appointed as trainer at Wakefield, having scored 11 tries in 99 appearances for the Rovers.

Ernie Barraclough, the stalwart prop forward who played from 1921 to 1934, made a record 435 appearances for a forward – which still stands today. He supposedly retired in 1934, but was retained on the club register and, when Broughton Rangers showed interest, was transferred for £100.

An early Rovers team photograph from 1923/24, with the Clayton Hospital (against Wakefield) and Lyon (against Castleford) Charity Cups. From left to right, back row: T. Ward, W. Clements, A. Haigh, J. Hirst, E. Barraclough, T. Wynard, N. Tait, V. Kinsey, J.W. Higson, W. Williams, G. Johnson. Middle row: J. McGlone, S. Denton, J. Denton, S. Woolley, P. Hepworth, A. Taylor, W. Seymour. Front row: J. Williams, F. Gill.

In 1926, the club obtained a loan of £1,500 from the Rugby League Council 'towards the cost of a stand to hold 2,000 spectators'. The total cost was £2,500, the club raising the balance. The stand was erected during the close season of 1926, watched by hundreds of out-of-work miners who sat on the field. The loan was to be repaid at £150 per year, but was not finally paid off until 1960, because of the severe financial difficulties in the 1930s and '40s.

14

Jack Hirst, described as the 'Prince of Centres', made 277 appearances, scoring 115 tries and 3 goals from 1921 to 1931. He was the first Rovers player to gain international honours (England *v.* Wales, 1923) and represented Yorkshire on 4 occasions. He would undoubtedly have added to these records but for injury, which caused his early retirement. He had a devastating swerve and side-step, scoring many memorable tries. In the Challenge Cup second round game with Wigan in March 1923, Wigan had taken an 11-0 lead after 30 minutes, when Hirst scored a great solo try to inspire the Rovers. Two tries by Les Mason enabled the Rovers to take the lead 13-11 well into the second half. Ring then put Wigan ahead with an unconverted try, 14-13, and in a breathtaking finale, Hirst had another try disallowed and J. Williams went over the line but dropped the ball. Wigan therefore, scraped through in front of a 10,000 crowd who had paid a total of £625 – records which were to exist for thirty years. Again in 1928, Hirst's memorable try at Huddersfield in the second round of the Yorkshire Cup gave the Rovers a 7-4 victory over the league leaders. Although they reached their first Yorkshire Cup final, the team was disappointedly beaten 5-0 by Leeds.

The Denton brothers, Jim (left) and Sid (below), were an integral part of the Rovers teams of the 1920s. Both were in the opening fixture at Bradford in August 1921, playing on the wings. Jim continued mainly as a winger for the rest of his career, which ended on 17 March 1933 in the home game against Dewsbury. In 440 appearances (which is still a club record), he amassed 1,141 points (129 tries, 377 goals) and topped the goal and points scoring lists in every season bar one from 1921 to 1934 – Ben Gronow temporarily replaced him in 1928/29. Jim also represented Yorkshire on four occasions.

Sid Denton settled into the fullback berth for most of his career, making 348 appearances, the last of which was at home to Hunslet on 17 September 1932. He scored 7 goals and 28 tries and is particularly remembered for his try against Leeds in the Top Four play-offs in 1928. Leeds were winning 10-7 when Sid raced 75 yards to score and the Rovers won 15-12. Sadly, in the Championship Final at Oldham, they gave an inept display to lose to Swinton 11-0, thus enabling the Lancashire club to achieve the rare distinction of four cups in the season.

16

# Chapter Two
# The 1930s

This decade was undoubtedly the worst in the Rover's history, and how the club survived is not only one of the greatest achievements in rugby league history, but also an inspiration to the less fortunate clubs in the game. By 1934, the club had lost Jack Hirst, the Denton brothers, and Jimmy Williams – players who had been the backbone of the side. The departure of these stalwarts left gaps which could not easily be filled, as the dire financial position of the club meant that any talented players were inevitably transferred to ease the situation. Such players included Billy Stott, George Johnson Jnr, Ernest Winter, Fred Smith, Cyril Plenderleith, Will Hayes, Johnny Malpass, Luke Morgan and Joe Evans.

Naturally, on-the-field performances suffered. From 1930 to 1937, the club was invariably in the bottom three and in two seasons had over 800 points scored against them – 804 in 1934/35 and 858 in 1936/37. In April 1934, the team won at Bramley and the next away league victory was not obtained until March 1937, when a 16-9 victory at Leigh ended a most unenviable record. The decline became a vicious spiral as plummeting attendances and severe economic depression, characterised by high unemployment, exacerbated the financial situation. To make matters worse, nearby Castleford were highly successful at this time. In April 1933, they came to Featherstone with a post-First World War record of 18 matches without defeat and won 25-0. The only comfort for the Rovers was a record league attendance of 9,334 – of whom 1,800 were unemployed and admitted for 6d.

There were no other such highlights. In March 1930 the lowest ever attendance of 200, who paid a total of 30s 8d, was recorded against Bradford and as the 1930s progressed, gate receipts dropped to less than £1,000 in a season. The situation was so serious that in January 1935, the Rugby League Council sent a deputation to ascertain the financial position.

How the Rovers survived those dark and stormy days was a credit to George Johnson and his fellow committeemen, who had to run a very economical ship. Mr Johnson's retirement in 1937 brought the crisis to a head, but the club was fortunate to secure a saviour in Mr Abe Bullock. He immediately launched a 5,000 shillings appeal fund, heading the contribution list with a personal gift of £50. A new policy was adopted by the committee, fourteen new players were signed, and only one player left the club. The reward was the best playing record since 1932 in 1938/39, including a shock win against Hunslet, the league leaders, 15-11. This raised hopes at the end of the decade that the corner had been turned, but then world events intervened.

|         | P  | W  | D | L  | For | Agst | Pts | Posn   |
|---------|----|----|---|----|-----|------|-----|--------|
| 1930/31 | 38 | 7  | 1 | 30 | 266 | 540  | 15  | 26(28) |
| 1931/32 | 38 | 15 | 2 | 21 | 374 | 415  | 32  | 19(28) |
| 1932/33 | 38 | 8  | 2 | 28 | 303 | 597  | 18  | 26(28) |
| 1933/34 | 38 | 4  | 0 | 34 | 232 | 734  | 8   | 28(28) |
| 1934/35 | 38 | 6  | 0 | 32 | 293 | 804  | 12  | 27(28) |
| 1935/36 | 38 | 5  | 4 | 29 | 269 | 625  | 14  | 29(30) |
| 1936/37 | 38 | 5  | 0 | 33 | 317 | 858  | 10  | 30(30) |
| 1937/38 | 36 | 8  | 2 | 26 | 311 | 606  | 18  | 26(29) |
| 1938/39 | 40 | 13 | 2 | 25 | 292 | 541  | 28  | 22(28) |

(With clubs all playing the same number of matches, the percentage system had ceased.)

Fred Norbury, Jack Hirst, George Whittaker, Ben Gronow and J.T. Morris. The now-familiar blue-and-white striped jerseys had yet to emerge. Apparently, the Rovers adopted blue and white in their junior club days but, to celebrate their entry into senior rugby league in 1921, changed to chocolate and white. They retained these colours until 1937, when they reverted to blue and white.

A Rovers team from the early 1930s. From left to right, back row: P. Morris, E. Winter, S. Denton, J. Morgan, M. Killingbeck, L. Morgan, F. Norbury, C. Flaherty. Front row: O. Darlison, G. Barker, W. Evans, J. Evans, -?-.

The Junction Hotel branch of the Supporters Club took over the club programme in 1933/34. This programme was for the Leigh game on 18 November 1933, which the Rovers won 8-5 (one of only four victories that season, as they finished bottom of the league). The club provided the full contents from 1955 and assumed total responsibility from 1966.

Membership cards were first issued in 1922. In 1934, the scheme was extended to local collieries for men to pay 3d per week for their cards. 700 joined at Ackton Hall Colliery and 300 at Featherstone Main. This remained a major contribution to the Rovers' finances until the demise of the coal industry in the 1980s.

In May 1935, Post Office Road staged a special match before the cameras as part of the film *The Hope of His Side*, starring Sidney Howard, a popular comedian of the day. Amongst the Rugby League stars participating (above) were: Jim Brough, Stan Brogden, Arthur Atkinson and Alex Fiddes. The Rovers players, shown with the officials (below), were: G. Taylor, H. Smith, P. Morris, P. Sutcliffe, R. Asquith, J. Malpass and G. Johnson Jnr. Sidney Howard scored the winning try and unemployed miners were paid 10s per day for crowd scenes.

| Payments | | £ | s | d |
|---|---|---|---|---|
| Players' Wages & Expenses | ... | 1012 | 15 | 5 |
| Bagman, Trainer & Groundsman | ... | 184 | 5 | 0 |
| Gatemen & Checkers | ... | 33 | 8 | 0 |
| Referees & Touch Judges | ... | 78 | 2 | 0 |
| Police | ... | 25 | 7 | 5 |
| Travelling Expenses | ... | 141 | 3 | 5 |
| Ground Expenses | ... | 30 | 17 | 9 |
| Tackle | ... | 11 | 10 | 0 |
| Stamps, Telephone & Stationery | ... | 20 | 18 | 10 |
| Meetings & Club Business | ... | 8 | 13 | 1 |
| Printing & Advertising | ... | 70 | 3 | 10 |
| Medical Sundries & Professional Charges | ... | 10 | 6 | 9 |
| Refreshments—Visiting Committees | ... | 13 | 6 | 0 |
| Entertainments Tax | ... | 166 | 8 | 10 |
| Players' Compensation | ... | 86 | 0 | 0 |
| Transfer & Inter-League Fees | ... | 40 | 0 | 0 |
| Fire Insurance—Stand | ... | 7 | 5 | 9 |
| Registration of Players | ... | 1 | 5 | 0 |
| Grants | ... | 8 | 18 | 0 |
| Salaries & Audit Fees | ... | 59 | 4 | 0 |
| Bank Charges | ... | 12 | 10 | 3 |
| Entrance Fees to League | ... | 7 | 7 | 0 |
| Wharncliffe Disaster Fund | ... | 3 | 0 | 0 |
| Lighting & Heating | ... | 20 | 11 | 9 |
| Rent & Rates | ... | 91 | 3 | 0 |
| National Health & Unemployment Insurance | ... | 7 | 19 | 8 |
| Sundries | ... | 3 | 17 | 9 |
| Cash in Secretary's hands | ... | | 18 | 7 |
| Cash in Bank | ... | 32 | 1 | 7 |
| | | £2189 | 8 | 8 |

| Liabilities | | | | |
|---|---|---|---|---|
| R. L. Loan £100 and Interest at 4% | ... | 128 | 0 | 0 |
| R. L. Loan £1350 and Interest at 4% | ... | 1728 | 0 | 0 |

Expenditure details from the statement of accounts for 1936/37. The main income was from gate receipts (£705), members' subscriptions and donations (£689), special efforts (£259) and a Supporters Club grant of £50.

An extract from the Rovers programme of 21 November 1936. The article followed the Rovers' narrow 19-16 defeat at Leeds on 31 October 1936.

# A FEW WORDS FROM " LITTLE JOHN "

by kind permission of the "Sports Post" (The White Paper)

WHEN approached to submit a few lines for your now excellent programme, I was really at a loss insomuch that there are so many different matters which could be discussed about R. L. football. After consideration I thought it best to draw attention to what others think about your team. After such appreciation surely the Featherstone public have no need to lose their enthusiasm, and I for one sincerely hope that in the near future Featherstone will occupy the position in the League to which such displays rightly entitle them.

## VOTE OF THANKS DUE

We have received the following letter from a Leeds Rugby League follower who signs himself "Moneys-Worth"

" I think a vote of thanks is due from the Headingley spectators to the Featherstone footballers for the splendid exhibition of the Rugby League game served up by them last Saturday. The pity of it was that these men only drew losing pay when they really were well worth winning money, even if they did lose. Such matches as this will do the game a world of good."

Featherstone played good football and were brave, ever so brave. Their fight against odds—the entire team had not cost the amount paid for the transfer of some of the Leeds forwards—was a good one, and there was rare promise in some of their work. On that form, at all events, the team's position in the League table does not do them anything like justice.

Some of their young backs shaped excellently. Dennis was a good full back—he roused the interest of the Leeds crowd as much as any man on the side—and their courage and football ability, ability that must serve the club well if they can be kept together, was shown in the fine passing move they made in the closing minutes when Leeds, after a very desperate fight, had snatched the lead again.

The way in which Featherstone keep going is one of the marvels of the game. Their total gate receipts last season were not two-thirds of the sum taken by Leeds when Wigen were at Headingley a week last Saturday, and yet the Rovers, who have learned well how to cut their coat according to their cloth, had a balance in hand at the end of it all.

The pity of it is that they are not able to reap adequately the harvest to which they are entitled. Ever since they entered the League they have had a struggle, and season by season they have been compelled to transfer men. Their men —backs and forwards, and the curious thing is that they have produced more backs than forwards in recent times—are scattered all over the Northern Rugby League.

Had they been able to keep the best of their men they must at some time or another have put their name on to one of the game's trophies. They have been very near it, on more than one occasion, and it ought not to be forgotten that once they beat Leeds in a League Championship semi-final. That was in 1928 when the Rovers in the final were beaten by Swinton, who by that victory completed the four cups feat. Since then Featherstone have had their backs to the wall, fighting all the way.

They were a smart looking lot when they took the field at Headingley in their blue and white jerseys—smarter in fact than many of the bigger and wealthier clubs. They may not have much money at Featherstone, but they have the right sort of pride, and on last week's showing they do turn their men out well.

**" Little John "**

Abe Bullock succeeded George Johnson as president in 1937, a position he held until his death in 1968. Apart from his leadership, the club and players benefited from his generosity in many ways. In 1938, he provided new terracing on the railway side and a new children's stand. He then replaced this with the Bullock Stand in 1949. (This has since been replaced by the RJB Stand.)

From 1934 to 1937, there were various attempts to establish the game in the capital. The Rovers played their first game in London in 1934, losing 22-8 to London Highfield under floodlights at the White City Stadium. During this period, they also played Acton and Willesden (twice) and Streatham (four times). Their only success was in this fixture against Streatham, which they won 21-11.

# Chapter Three

# The 1940s

When war was declared in September 1939, the new season was immediately suspended and initially the Government banned all gatherings for the purpose of entertainment. This was soon rescinded and it was agreed to introduce the War Emergency League. A special meeting of the club was convened on 17 September, attended by 200 members, to discuss the future of Featherstone Rovers. The club was £600 in debt and it was essential that this did not worsen. The meeting acknowledged that if the Rovers folded it would not be revived, and it was decided to carry on, with the members present agreeing to pay their subscriptions whether football was played or not.

The War Emergency League initially consisted of two divisions, Lancashire and Yorkshire, but from 1941/42 it was decided to revert to one combined league. Many clubs used guest players during the war, but the Rovers playing strength consisted mainly of miners, who were exempt from war service, and only fourteen guest players were used. Inevitably, fixture lists were disrupted through war restrictions.

When peace-time football was resumed in 1945, the Rovers were heartened with their best playing season since 1928. Average gate receipts improved to £128 and with promising young talent, prospects looked good. The 'A' team, which had been revived in 1939, won both the Yorkshire Senior Competition League and Cup competitions. Regrettably, the promise was not fulfilled, and with the premature retirement through injury of inspirational scrum-half Jack Higgins, results and attendances suffered. In 1946/47, only one win was recorded in seventeen games, but then the league leaders Widnes were defeated 3-2 in a titanic struggle at Post Office Road. With finances reaching crisis levels again, players had to be sold and an Appeal Fund for £1,000 was launched. In April 1949, Huddersfield supporters paid the Rovers' travelling expenses for the game at Huddersfield as 'a tribute to the great efforts made by the Featherstone club to keep the Rugby League flag flying in face of difficulties'.

It was a depressingly familiar story, but the turn in fortune came at the end of 1949, when the club made the most astute signings of the post-war era with the arrival of Don Graham and Freddie Miller. Miller's debut brought the first win for twelve matches and, although an enthusiastic cup run ended at Barrow in the second round, a new spirit prevailed in the camp at the dawn of the 1950s.

| War Emergency Yorkshire | P | W | D | L | Pts For | Agst | Pts | Posn |
|---|---|---|---|---|---|---|---|---|
| 1939/40 | 28 | 15 | 0 | 13 | 373 | 365 | 30 | 7(15) |
| 1940/41 | 24 | 14 | 0 | 10 | 255 | 255 | 28 | 7(14) |
| **War Emergency League** | | | | | | | | |
| 1941/42 | 18 | 8 | 0 | 10 | 166 | 181 | 16 | 12(17) |
| 1942/43 | 19 | 10 | 1 | 8 | 179 | 138 | 21 | 8(14) |
| 1943/44 | 22 | 6 | 0 | 16 | 202 | 229 | 12 | 13(16) |
| 1944/45 | 22 | 8 | 0 | 14 | 153 | 229 | 16 | 14(17) |
| **End of Emergency** | | | | | | | | |
| 1945/46 | 36 | 19 | 1 | 16 | 407 | 395 | 39 | 13(27) |
| 1946/47 | 36 | 9 | 1 | 26 | 217 | 477 | 19 | 26(28) |
| 1947/48 | 36 | 6 | 0 | 30 | 270 | 724 | 12 | 27(28) |
| 1948/49 | 36 | 9 | 3 | 24 | 305 | 519 | 21 | 26(29) |
| 1949/50 | 36 | 9 | 2 | 25 | 299 | 550 | 20 | 25(29) |

The Rovers secured their first trophy in senior football on 22 June 1940, when they defeated Wakefield Trinity 12-9 in the Yorkshire Cup final at Odsal. The competition had been deferred from the beginning of the season in 1939 because of the outbreak of war. The first round was played on 1 June 1940, and the Rovers were favoured with home draws through to the final. Halifax were disposed of 18-2 in the first round, and the major shock was the victory over Bradford, the Yorkshire Champions, 21-6 in the second round. A 15-11 semi-final win over Dewsbury paved the way to the final. The Rovers' scored through tries by Walt Tennant and Albany Longley and three goals by Bill Sherwood. The attendance was 7,077 with gate receipts of £403. From left to right, back row: W. Williams (trainer), J. Dyson, F. Hemingway, G. Taylor, J. Golby, A. Longley, W. Jackson, J. Haley, A. Bullock (president). Middle row: J. Blackburn, W. Hughes, W. Pearson (captain), W. Sherwood, W. Tennant. Front row: R. Hamer, H. Moxon.

A Rovers side from 1939/40. From left to right, back row: W. Jackson, J. Pollitt, A. Jacobs, F. Dyson, J. Golby, G. Taylor, W. Pearson, F. Hemingway. Front row: W. Parkin, W. Hughes, H. Moxon, L. Davis, W. Tennant. Note the new Children's Stand in the background.

Featherstone's junior production line is legendary. The players in this 1947/48 Intermediates team are, from left to right, back row: P. Newton, C. Lambert, J. Evans, K. Hill, R. Reynolds, D. Newsome. Front row: ? Morgan, D. Davies, G. Hanson, A. Tennant, D. Hill, R. Evans, -?-. Newton, Lambert, Reynolds, Davies, Tennant and Evans all progressed to the Rovers' senior team, together with an absent member of this team, Willis Fawley.

The Featherstone Rovers team that lost 32-0 to Hunslet in an away game on 16 October 1948. From left to right, back row: F. Richardson, D. Smith, J. Stephenson, M. Kent, L. Mogg, T. Townsend, H. Lyman. Front row: F. Church, L. Gant, E. Davis, W. Best (captain), J. Russell, W. Allinson.

Rovers team for the Challenge Cup first-round, second-leg game against Swinton on 19 February 1949. From left to right, back row: F. Richardson, T. Townsend, J. Stephenson, F. Bolton, K. Welburn, M. Kent, W. Allinson. Front row: F. Church, R. Allman, W. Tennant, J. Russell, J. Ogden, T. Crabtree. Rovers won this encounter 13-10 but lost on aggregate 25-15. The two-leg system for the first round was introduced in 1941 and discontinued in 1955.

Don Graham was the first colonial to play for Featherstone. He was acquired short-term from Hunslet in a sporting gesture in December 1949, before returning to Australia. He was appointed captain and, although only playing nine games, inspired a mini-cup run and endeared himself to all during his brief stay. He died three years later at the tragically young age of thirty-one.

The Rovers team that lost 6-0 at home to Bradford on 24 September 1949. From left to right, back row: E. Davis, R. Reynolds, K. Welburn, A. Wood, T. Townsend, F. Hemingway, L. Payne, M. Kent. Front row: D. Altass, L. Gant, J. Blackburn, J. Russell, W. Tennant, C. Gilbertson, T. Crabtree, C. Lambert. This was Walt Tennant's last season. He had been signed from Girnhill Lane in August 1939, and his peerless centre play was reminiscent of 1920s star Jack Hirst. He had a brief transfer to Wakefield Trinity in 1946 (nine months) and scored 104 tries for the Rovers in 234 appearances.

A seemingly impromptu team photograph from late 1949. Coach Bill Sherwood is on the left and amongst players identified on back row are: Brian Kelly, Arthur Wood, Les Payne, Cliff Lambert, Willis Fawley, George Major (in overcoat). Middle row: Frank Hemingway, Jack Blackburn, Walt Tennant, Fred Church, Bob Jarvis. Front row: Jimmy Russell, Frank Bolton, Laurie Gant. Frank Hemingway made his senior debut in November 1934 and played his final game in September 1950, having made 361 appearances over sixteen years. Laurie Gant was acquired from Wakefield in March 1948 and immediately helped to halt a disastrous 24-match losing spell which had lasted since November 1947, with a rare 12-8 win at Hull KR in April.

# Chapter Four

# The 1950s

After enduring the particularly dark days of the 1930s and '40s, it was appropriate that the dedication of the Rovers' support should at last be rewarded with the most successful decade since the club's elevation to senior status. Yet not even the most ardent supporter could have dreamed how the 1950s would unfold.

The spark was innocuously provided by three of the most astute signings in the club's history. It seems extravagant to highlight the effect of the signing of a player who only appeared in nine games at the beginning of 1950, but the acquisition of Don Graham from Hunslet was extremely influential. He was an inspirational player who instilled a new spirit into the young Rovers team of that time. The momentum was then carried on by Freddie Miller, whose goal-kicking exploits and experience brought their own transformation. The signing of another veteran, Eric Batten, completed the trio, and Batten's influence as player-coach, with his emphasis on fitness, was paramount. It was the blending of this experience with the youthful talent that was available which sparked the famous Wembley run of 1952 and upon which the rest of the decade was built.

Having experienced Wembley in 1952, there was perhaps disappointment that the team was not able to progress beyond the semi-final stage in 1955, 1958 and 1959, but these runs were still magnificent achievements forever etched in the memories of those who witnessed them and in the annals of the game. In addition, there was the success in the 1959 Yorkshire Cup final and the general improvement in league positions – culminating in the Rovers' best-ever league record in 1959/60. At the end of the decade, Featherstone Rovers were undoubtedly capable of competing with the best in rugby league. Linked with this was probably one of the most productive eras of the Featherstone junior conveyer belt, which excelled itself in consistently unearthing outstanding talent. Many of the great Rovers players belong to this era, and they were the product of both this system and some astute transfer activity. The resulting increase in attendances was richly deserved.

|  | P | W | D | L | Pts For | Agst | Pts | Posn |
|---|---|---|---|---|---|---|---|---|
| 1950/51 | 36 | 12 | 1 | 23 | 375 | 562 | 25 | 26(29) |
| 1951/52 | 36 | 14 | 2 | 20 | 431 | 470 | 30 | 22(31) |
| 1952/53 | 36 | 12 | 1 | 23 | 415 | 535 | 25 | 24(30) |
| 1953/54 | 36 | 18 | 2 | 16 | 478 | 431 | 38 | 14(30) |
| 1954/55 | 36 | 23 | 1 | 12 | 572 | 424 | 47 | 9(31) |
| 1955/56 | 36 | 23 | 2 | 11 | 579 | 464 | 48 | 6(30) |
| 1956/57 | 38 | 19 | 0 | 19 | 612 | 504 | 38 | 15(30) |
| 1957/58 | 38 | 23 | 1 | 14 | 608 | 497 | 47 | 8(30) |
| 1958/59 | 38 | 18 | 3 | 17 | 597 | 613 | 39 | 13(30) |
| 1959/60 | 38 | 27 | 0 | 11 | 730 | 437 | 54 | 5(30) |

Action from the Challenge Cup first-round, second-leg tie at Bramley in February 1950. The Rovers players are: A. Wood (9), L. Gant (12), K. Welburn (10) and L. Payne (14). Arthur Wood was signed in 1947, played for Yorkshire and England in 1950/51, and was transferred to Leeds for a then record transfer fee of £3,000 in 1951. He made 105 appearances for the Rovers.

Controversy surrounded the Yorkshire Cup first-round encounter with Bradford in September 1951. Played over two legs, Rovers won 4-2 at home but lost 11-9 at Bradford. With the scores level, both clubs refused to play extra time as they considered the light would have failed and Bradford won the replay at Wakefield 17-9. The Yorkshire County Committee then confiscated the gate receipts and fined both clubs £50 for not playing extra time. In this action shot from the game at Wakefield, Laurie Gant kicks ahead watched by Jimmy Russell.

After a long and distinguished career with Hull, which began in 1932, Freddie Miller was transferred to the Rovers in January 1950 for £200. He made his debut at home to Whitehaven and kicked two goals (one a drop goal from half-way), inspiring the Rovers to their first win in 12 games. A prodigious kicker, he broke the club goal-scoring record in 1950/51 with 97 goals, and promptly bettered this with 101 goals in the glorious Wembley season of 1952. His influential full-back play inspired his team on many occasions. His last game was against Dewsbury in November 1952 at the age of thirty-six, and he kicked two goals to bring his remarkable Rovers career record to 92 appearances, 245 goals and 2 tries (a total of 496 points).

With the transfer money for Wood (£3,000) and Payne (£1,500 from Dewsbury), the club bought Paddy Daly, Maurice Ogden, Alan Sinclair and Eric Batten. The signing of Batten, together with that of Freddie Miller, was inspired. Both players were considered past their sell-by-date when they joined the Rovers. Batten came as player-coach at the age of thirty-five and his style of coaching was fitness, allied with highly coordinated and organised defence and backed by burning spirit and enthusiasm. He scored on his Rovers debut against Rochdale at home in August 1951, and broke the club try-scoring record with 26 in 1952/53. He ceased playing in September 1954, having scored 60 tries in 101 games – testimony to his own personal fitness. He resigned as coach in 1956. This photograph shows him scoring his 400th try in the 1952 Cup game with Wigan.

Two great Rovers Challenge Cup teams that faced Wigan, in 1923 and 1952. From left to right, back row: W. Williams, E. Barraclough, E. Richardson, W. Morrell, T. Wynard, E. Woolley, A. Haigh, W. Clements, C. Hepworth, H. Goodall, F. Miller, F. Hulme. Middle row (seated): J. Denton, J. Hirst, W. Seymour, J. Williams, J. Kirkham, L. Mason. Front row: C. Lambert, R. Cording, R. Evans, K. Welburn, W. Bradshaw, A. Tennant, E. Batten, D. Metcalfe, L. Gant, P. Daly, N. Mitchell. This photograph was taken on 15 March 1952, when the Rovers entertained Wigan in the third round of the Challenge Cup. A record crowd of 14,344 (receipts £2,308), witnessed one of the most memorable games played at Post Office Road. At 2-2, Cliff Lambert blundered to let Hilton in for a try, but the young loose forward soon atoned for this mistake when he broke away to send Mitchell under the posts, Miller's conversion giving the Rovers a 7-5 interval lead. More thrills followed in the second half as the Rovers' terrier-like tactics harassed the Wigan stars, and two towering drop goals by Freddie Miller increased their advantage. Wigan hit back with a second try by Hilton, but Eric Batten went over to restore the lead at 14-8. As Wigan tried to save the game, Miller's ponderous kicking and tremendous team efforts kept them out. Nordgren scored a late try but Rovers' 14-11 win signified the biggest post-war shock in Challenge Cup circles.

The 1952 Challenge Cup heroes (above) and the jubilant fans (below). It was estimated that the Rovers had a following of 10,000 supporters in this Cup run; the average league attendance that season was 3,800.

The 1952 Challenge Cup exploits continued with a 6-2 semi-final win over Leigh in front of 35,000 spectators at Headingley. The action shots show (above) Cliff Lambert breaking away from the scrum, shadowed by Ray Evans, who nearly scored himself (below). Three golden goals by Freddie Miller were decisive.

The 1952 squad line-up at their Westcliffe-on-Sea headquarters. From left to right: W. Bradshaw, L. Gant, R. Evans, A. Tennant, R. Cording, J. Ogden, F. Miller, N. Mitchell, K. Welburn, K. Goulding, E. Batten, J. Daly, D. Metcalfe, F. Hulme, C. Lambert.

Bob Jackson, the Featherstone Rovers chairman, leads the team out at Wembley on 19 April 1952. Note the uncovered section of the famous stadium in those days.

In what was described as the most thrilling final at Wembley since the war, Workington won 18-10 before a crowd of 73,000 (receipts £22,374). Seven points down in the first quarter, two towering goals by Miller reduced the deficit for Rovers. Just after the interval, Batten scored a memorable try (below) to level the scores. Mudge then gave Workington the lead before the most decisive and disheartening moment of the game. The Rovers broke through and with a two-man overlap seemed certain to score, but Daly's pass was intercepted by Lawrenson, the Workington winger, who raced 70 yards to touch down under the posts. Ray Evans scored a last-minute consolation try. Eric Batten, Rovers captain, was appearing in his fourth Wembley Challenge Cup final as he had been in the Bradford Northern teams of 1947, 1948 and 1949.

THE RUGBY LEAGUE CHALLENGE CUP COMPETITION

# FINAL TIE

**FEATHERSTONE v WORKINGTON
ROVERS TOWN**

SATURDAY, APRIL 19th, 1952 KICK-OFF 3pm

**The Empire Stadium
WEMBLEY**

Chairman and Managing Director: SIR ARTHUR J. ELVIN, M.B.E.

OFFICIAL PROGRAMME · ONE SHILLING

Rovers had beaten Rochdale in the two-leg first round (8-7 away and 17-2 at home) and Batley 11-4 (away) in the second round, before their encounters with Wigan and Leigh. Prior to the final they scored 56 points with 26 against, with 16 goals by Freddie Miller.

The welcome home for Featherstone's defeated heroes.

Bob Jackson, the Featherstone chairman, presents a cheque for £50 to Joe Mullaney for his first Yorkshire County appearance and international caps to Mick Clamp and Don Fox, who played for England Under 21 *v.* France at Avignon in the same year, 1954.

At last a fixture was fulfilled against a New Zealand Rugby League touring team. The Kiwis were scheduled to visit Featherstone in 1926, but the game was cancelled because, with the General Strike affecting the area, it was considered that it would not be profitable; the fixture in 1939 was cancelled because of the outbreak of war. On this occasion the Kiwis won 7-6, the attendance was 5,100 and receipts £650.

OFFICIAL SOUVENIR PROGRAMME—PRICE 6d.

**FEATHERSTONE ROVERS R.L.F.C.**

**Wednesday 19th October 1955**

**ROVERS**

**NEW ZEALAND**

Nº 2110

The Rovers side that beat Dewsbury 27-12 in an away game on 10 September 1955. From left to right, back row: W. Bradshaw, J. Barraclough, W. Shreeve, F. Hulme, K. Elford, P. Fox, M. Kirk. Front row: P. Johnson, D. Metcalfe, T. Smales, J. Fennell, R. Cording, M. Clamp.

Ken Welburn, Rovers' prop forward, scores against Leeds at Headingley in April 1956, encouraged by Cliff Lambert. In the background is Arthur Wood, the former Featherstone hooker. Ken made his senior debut at Hull on 20 November 1948 and his last match was against Bradford at home in April 1958. He made 263 appearances and scored 12 tries. His try at Leeds was the only one he scored away from home.

A famous 7-6 victory at Hull in September 1955 in the Yorkshire Cup first round – the Rovers' first victory at the Boulevard since 1933. Fennell and Metcalfe are pictured stopping Markham, the Hull forward, short of the line.

Rovers were not beaten by the mighty Wigan at Post Office Road in the 1950s. Apart from the 1952 Cup win, there were league victories in 1955 (13-6), 1956 (15-9) and 1958 (13-6). A Wigan attack is repulsed in the 1958 encounter, with Cliff Lambert and Ron Bradley close at hand.

A cartoonist's impression of Albert Fearnley, who was a member of the famous Halifax pack of the early 1950s and who was transferred to Featherstone in September 1957 for £750. His wholehearted efforts and enthusiasm made him a favourite with the fans, and in two years he made 67 appearances, scoring 18 tries and 2 goals – a record of which he was particularly proud. He left in August 1958 to be player-coach at Batley, and immediately plotted Rovers' downfall in a first-round Yorkshire Cup tie, Batley winning 21-5.

Frank Smith became Rovers costliest signing from rugby union in January 1957. Here he puts pen to paper, watched by committeemen John Jepson and Charlie Raybould and secretary Ron Bailey. At 6ft 4in and 14st 10lbs, he made his debut at home to Hunslet on 26 January, was concussed in a heavy tackle and spent the next two nights in Pontefract Infirmary. Nicknamed 'Cheyenne', he scored 52 tries in 101 appearances, before giving up the game somewhat prematurely in 1960.

Mr and Mrs A. Bullock officially open the new committee and refreshment rooms, secretary's office and players' dressing rooms before the Wigan match on 2 March 1957.

The Rovers heralded the start to the 1957/58 season with an impressive 20-12 Bullock Cup victory over Wakefield at Belle Vue. Cliff Lambert is shown scoring one of the Rovers tries, watched by Frank Smith, Mick Clamp and Albert Fearnley. Little did the Rovers faithful among the crowd know that more famous cup victories lay ahead.

George Potts, who reported Rovers affairs for many years, interviewing, from left to right: Abe Bullock (president), Ron Bailey (secretary), John Jepson (vice chairman), Bob Jackson (chairman), and Bessie Major (Ladies Committee), during 'A Spotlight on Featherstone Rovers' for the BBC North programme *Sporting Diary* on 8 November 1957.

League action at Derwent Park in December 1957, as Jack Fennell and Alan Marchant stop Ike Southward, the Workington winger. Workington were admitted to the League in 1945 and had a jinx hold over the Rovers. In eight League encounters to 1957, the Rovers only won one game, while in the Challenge Cup the Cumbrians had thwarted Rovers in the 1952 final (18-10), 1955 semi-final (13-2), and, three months after this win, another semi-final (8-2) in 1958.

The Featherstone and Swinton teams observe a minute's silence for the victims of the Manchester United air disaster at Munich, before their first-round Challenge Cup tie at Swinton on 8 February 1958. Rovers won 9-6.

The Rovers side that lost 21-0 away to Halifax on 15 March 1958. From left to right, back row: K. Welburn, H. Street, W. Jones, L. Evans, F. Smith, A. Fearnley. Front row: A. Marchant, C. Woolford, C. Lambert, W. Fawley, J. Mullaney, J. Fennell, A. Tennant.

We're on our way! Frank Smith scores in the corner during the 9-5 Challenge Cup second-round victory over Barrow in front of a 9,000 crowd at Post Office Road in 1958.

The Rovers team that beat Keighley away 27-12 in March 1958. From left to right, back row: H. Street, L. Evans, M. Dixon, F. Smith, W. Jones, D. Fox. Front row: R. Bell, C. Woolford, M. Clamp, C. Lambert, S. Moyser, A. Tennant, J. Fennell.

8 March 1958, and the Rovers produce another Challenge Cup shock as they beat favourites St Helens 5-0 in an epic encounter at Post Office Road. The match was played in a snowstorm. *Above:* Cliff Lambert scores the solitary try, having been put through by Harry Street. *Below:* The nearest Saints came to scoring as Van Vollenhoven is stopped by Les Evans, Joe Mullaney and Alan Marchant, with Willis Fawley on hand.

Some of the record crowd of 15,700 who braved the Arctic conditions to watch the St Helens game. Their courage was, in part, fortified by the contents of sixty-two empty whisky bottles, which were collected after the game by groundsman Bill Swallow!

Determined efforts by Cyril Woolford, Harry Street and Joe Mullaney in the 1958 Challenge Cup semi-final, but Workington triumphed 8-2 in the Odsal mud. A crowd of 31,715 watched this match.

League action at Knowsley Road against St Helens in August 1958 as Brian Kinsey, Rovers winger, attempts to beat his renowned opponent, Tom Van Vollenhoven. Other Rovers players, from left to right, are: Roy Bell, Mick Reynolds, Willis Fawley, Frank Moore, Cliff Lambert. Ironically, twenty-seven years later, divisional officer Brian Kinsey was the fire service officer who attended when Rovers' main stand burned down in February 1985.

The Rovers team that beat Leeds 15-13 at home on 28 March 1959. From left to right, back row: T. Clawson, W. Fawley, C. Woolford, N. Hockley, W. Jones, G. Cooper, J. Anderson. Front row: F. Smith, M. Clamp, J. Mullaney, K. Greatorex, A. Marchant, J. Hunt.

The sceptics attributed St Helen's shock Challenge Cup defeat in 1958 to the atrocious weather conditions. When fate decreed that the two sides should again meet at the same stage of the competition at Featherstone a year later, experts again forecasted a Saints victory. In ideal conditions, the Rovers completely outplayed their opponents, securing an even more emphatic 20-6 victory. Skipper Joe Mullaney (number six, above) and Norman Hockley (number twelve, below) scored two of the tries in front of a crowd of 17,351 (yielding receipts of £3,454). The attendance record still remains and is unlikely to be broken with the present reduced ground capacity.

One of the pleasing features of the 1959 Challenge Cup campaign was the breaking of the Workington jinx. The Rovers gained their first League win at Workington on 14 February and returned the following week to record their first Challenge Cup victory in an 8-5 first-round encounter. With Workington disposed of, the Rovers were extremely hopeful of winning their semi-final clash with Hull on 11 April, but their dreams were again dashed in the Odsal bowl. The emphasis during the game was mainly on defence, as depicted in these action shots, and Hull won a dour match 15-5 in front of a 52,500 crowd.

The Rovers team that beat Keighley 17-16 away on 19 September 1959. From left to right, back row: F. Moore, K. Kingsbury, E. Broom, M. Dixon, W. Fawley, D. Fox, T. Clawson. Front row: G. Cooper, M. Clamp, J. Mullaney (captain), C. Woolford, J. Hunt, F. Smith.

The Rovers team that beat Hunslet 20-5 at home on 24 October 1959. From left to right, back row: W. Fawley, D. Fox, T. Clawson, C. Lambert, J. Fennell, M. Dixon, J. Anderson. Front row: F. Smith, C. Woolford, M. Clamp, J. Mullaney (captain), A. Tennant, K. Greatorex.

In the 1959 Yorkshire Cup, Rovers reached the final with an uninspiring 14-7 home win over Leeds before a 10,700 crowd. Both sides were guilty of handling errors. Here, Cyril Woolford prepares to hand-off Quinn, the Leeds full-back.

The delight of Rovers' success in the Yorkshire Cup was tinged with sadness by the resignation of chairman Bob Jackson prior to the Leeds match. He had served on the committee since 1937, being elected chairman in 1950. His generosity helped the club out of many financial difficulties, and as Rovers' representative on the Rugby League Council and Yorkshire County Committee, he furthered the standing of the club in Rugby League circles. In 1956, he was chairman of the Yorkshire County Committee, being the first Featherstone official to hold such a post. He later returned to the committee and was elected president in 1968.

YORKSHIRE COUNTY RUGBY LEAGUE

**CHALLENGE CUP FINAL**

—1959—

**FEATHERSTONE R. v. HULL**

SATURDAY
31st OCTOBER
1959

Kick-off 3.0 p.m.

At HEADINGLEY
LEEDS

**OFFICIAL SOUVENIR PROGRAMME - Price 6d.**

The 15-14 victory over Hull in the Yorkshire Cup final was sweet revenge for the Challenge Cup semi-final defeat earlier in the year, and was the first peace-time trophy won by the club. Ten of the Rovers thirteen had been signed from junior football.

Don Fox opened the scoring after 5 minutes, despite the efforts of Johnny Whiteley and Bill Drake. Terry Clawson, Joe Anderson, Malcom Dixon and Cliff Lambert are pictured awaiting the referee's confirmation, but Willis Fawley is already showing his jubilation.

56

After a try by Whiteley had given Hull a 7-5 lead, the Rovers hit a purple patch later in the first half with tries by Cliff Lambert (above) and Cyril Woolford. This gave them a 13-7 interval lead, and their excellent defence withstood a strong second-half rally from Hull.

A happy post-match dressing room.

The Rovers gained their first victory over an Australian touring team on 11 November 1959. The 23-15 win was a classic game, watched by a crowd of 7,600. *Above:* Don Fox scores. *Below:* The Rovers defence matched their attacking efforts, as Frank Smith demonstrates with Ken Greatorex in attendance. After the game, the Aussies described the Rovers as the best club side they had played.

# Chapter Five

# The 1960s

The momentum gained in the 1950s was carried into the early part of the 1960s. There were nine new club records created in 1959/60, but it was the Challenge Cup that continued to inspire Rovers. Semi-final appearances in 1960 and 1962, followed by a controversial exit at the third round stage in 1961, continued a remarkable sequence. It meant that in the 25 stages of the Challenge Cup from 1958 to 1962, Featherstone had participated in 19 and had recorded some magnificent victories against the best sides in rugby league, both home and away. With a record 57 points in the League to finish third, 1961/62 was possibly the best season ever, but Championship hopes were again thwarted at the semi-final stage.

Naturally, there was some frustration and disappointment at being so near but yet so far, and, when the club's fortunes dipped in the mid-1960s, the warning bells sounded. The retirement of stalwarts Joe Mullaney, Jack Fennell, Colin Clifft and Willis Fawley, and the departure of Don Fox, Terry Clawson, Ivor Lingard and Terry Ramshaw were significant – the spectre of having to sell to survive had returned. In 1965/66, a mediocre season by Rovers' recent standards, League attendances totalled 45,625 with average receipts of £134 – the lowest peace-time total since 1938/39 – and in 1966/67 the average was only £227.

Yet in the season of their worst League record of the decade, Rovers reached their first pinnacle with yet another outstanding, but this time successful, Challenge Cup campaign. Laurie Gant, appointed coach in 1966, masterminded the Wembley success in 1967. Better Rovers teams had failed in the past, but the spirit and dedication he instilled in this side triumphed.

|  | P | W | S | L | Pts For | Agst | Pts | Posn |
|---|---|---|---|---|---|---|---|---|
| 1960/61 | 36 | 23 | 1 | 11 | 520 | 403 | 47 | 9(30) |
| 1961/62 | 36 | 28 | 1 | 7 | 621 | 370 | 57 | 3(30) |
| 1962/63 | 30 | 12 | 3 | 15 | 389 | 407 | 27 | 11(16) |
| 1963/64 | 30 | 18 | 1 | 11 | 485 | 364 | 37 | 4(16) |
| 1964/65 | 34 | 18 | 0 | 16 | 436 | 463 | 36 | 15(30) |
| 1965/66 | 34 | 17 | 0 | 17 | 408 | 399 | 34 | 15(30) |
| 1966/67 | 34 | 12 | 3 | 19 | 401 | 477 | 27 | 20(30) |
| 1967/68 | 34 | 16 | 0 | 18 | 455 | 437 | 32 | 18(30) |
| 1968/69 | 34 | 21 | 1 | 12 | 523 | 346 | 43 | 7(30) |

(A First Division operated in 1962/63 and 1963/64.)

There was more Challenge Cup glory in 1960 with a highly impressive away victory sequence against leading clubs. The first round brought a 15-0 win at Workington, the second round was won 16-10 in a white-hot encounter at Halifax, and then Rovers triumphed 11-7 in the third round at Swinton. *Above:* Frank Smith scores in the match against Halifax. *Below:* Referee Eric Clay prepares to confirm Willis Fawley's try in the Swinton game.

The Rovers team that faced Swinton in the Challenge Cup on 19 March 1960. From left to right, back row: J. Anderson, T. Clawson, M. Dixon, F. Smith, C. Clifft, C. Lambert. Front row: J. Fennell, D. Fox, K. Greatorex, J. Mullaney, W. Fawley, J. Hunt, C. Woolford.

A third successive Challenge Cup semi-final appearance in 1960 again brought frustration, as Wakefield won 11-2 in front of 55,800 spectators at Odsal Stadium, Bradford. A deciding moment in the first half was when Lambert kicked through for Mullaney, only for the ball to bounce cruelly away from him over the line.

Cliff Lambert received a then record testimonial cheque of £535 from chairman John Jepson in the close season of 1961. Described by many as the finest ball-playing forward never to gain representative honours, Cliff's skilful play made tries for countless Rovers players, and he scored a few himself (83 in fact), during a career which commenced in the centre on 20 September 1949 at Batley (when he scored a debut try), and ended in the Championship semi-final at Wakefield on 5 May 1962. He made 376 appearances and, in a remarkable record of consistency, was a member of the Rovers Challenge Cup teams of 1952, 1955, 1958, 1960, 1961 and 1962. He only missed the 1959 side because of a cartilage operation. In 1953/54, he headed the Rugby League forwards' try-scoring lists with 13. He transferred to Hunslet in the close season of 1962.

In 1961, Rovers were thwarted in reaching the Challenge Cup semi-final for the fourth successive season with a highly controversial exit. Once again, the competition had inspired the team to great heights and after an 11-5 first round win at Keighley, the Rovers gained a magnificent 13-10 victory at Warrington. They then had the daunting task of visiting the Boulevard in the third round, but with two minutes remaining Rovers were winning 9-7. A touch judge then entered the field of play with his flag raised as Hollindrake, the Hull winger, received a pass and set off down the wing. Barry Charlesworth (shown with Terry Clawson and Gary Cooper in this action shot from the game), deflected him into touch. With no touch judge on the line, this was not confirmed by an official and Hollindrake continued to score in the corner. The referee, K. Rathbone, consulted with the touch judge but then awarded the try, stating that the touch judge was reporting an incident by a Featherstone player – Hull had won 10-9. Rovers protested to the Rugby League Council over the whole affair, but to no avail.

Freddie Miller, who made such an impact in the early 1950s, died on 20 July 1960 at the age of forty-five. A lasting tribute to his memory was unveiled on 22 April 1961, prior to the game with St Helens, when his widow, Mrs Nan Miller, received the keys to the Freddie Miller Memorial Gate from Cliff Lambert. Freddie served two clubs with distinction, Rovers and Hull, and it was appropriate that officials from Hull were present at the ceremony.

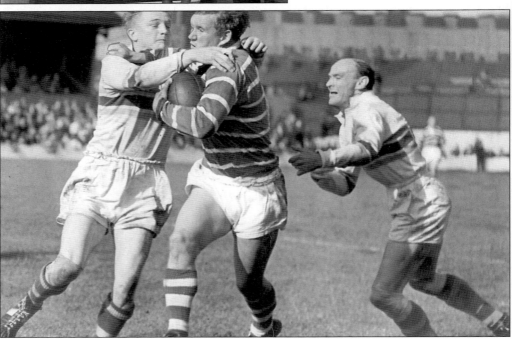

A fine action shot from the early 1960s as Jim Hunt, the Rovers centre, comes to grips with Warrington stars Brian Bevan and Jim Challinor (who was later a member of the Barrow Cup final team in 1967).

One of the Rovers' greatest wingers retired in April 1961. Cyril Woolford had joined the club five years earlier in April 1956 from Doncaster for a mere £400 at the age of twenty-eight. He made his debut against Leeds at home on 7 April 1956, and scored two tries in the 35-16 win. He appeared in 185 of the 217 games played by Rovers from then until 19 April 1961, when he played his last game in the home match with Batley. He scored 88 tries and set up a club try-scoring record of 31 in 1958/59. His wholehearted endeavour, combined with tenacity in defence and forcefulness in attack, left a lasting impression, and it seemed an injustice that such efforts were not rewarded with a Wembley appearance in the Challenge Cup runs from 1958 to 1961 – but oh, how he tried! Here, he beats Billy Boston and Fred Griffiths in a League encounter with Wigan, although the referee ruled no try.

The Rovers team that lost 18-4 at home to Wakefield on 20 January 1962. From left to right, back row: G. Waterworth, C. Clifft, C. Lambert, T. Clawson, D. Fox, G. Jordan, L. Hammill. Front row: W. Fawley, J. Mullaney, K. Greatorex, N. Hockley, J. Fennell, J. Hunt. The only consolation in this defeat was a huge League attendance of 14,990 – which is still a record.

Gary Waterworth had a meteoric rise to fame. Signed in August 1961 from Roundhay Rugby Union, he scored three tries upon his debut against Dewsbury in September, was selected for Yorkshire v. Lancashire in October, again scoring on debut, and was then reserve winger for the Tests against New Zealand – all in the first four months of his senior career. With his electrifying pace, he was a star in the making but, regrettably, he gave up the game in 1964, having scored 33 tries in 68 appearances.

A programme from a unique event – a combined Rovers/Castleford team which lost to the touring Kiwis 31-20. The combined side was: A. Lunn (Castleford), K. Greatorex (Rovers), J. Hunt (Rovers), G. Ward (Castleford), C. Battye (Castleford), A. Hardisty (Castleford), D. Fox (Rovers), L. Hammill (Rovers), W. Fawley (Rovers), M. Dixon (Rovers), T. Clawson (Rovers), N. Hockley (Rovers), J. Sheridan (Castleford). Tries were scored by Ward (2), Hunt, and Hammill, while Clawson kicked four goals.

Harold Moxon, Rovers coach, congratulates Gary Waterworth and Len Hammill upon their selection for Yorkshire on 9 October 1961. Moxon was coach from 1958 to 1963 and, as such, was one of the most successful. He himself played for the Rovers from 1938 to 1946, making 112 appearances. He later recalled that the most tragic game he played in was the home game against Wakefield on 28 September 1946. Frank Townsend, the Wakefield centre, was tackled and carried from the field. He died three hours later and death by misadventure was recorded at the inquest.

Back on the Challenge Cup trail in 1962, Post Office Road witnessed another epic in March against Leigh. Rovers won 23-9 in front of 11,100 people. *Above:* Don Fox acclaims Cliff Lambert's try. *Below:* The Rovers team, from left to right, back row: G. Waterworth, T. Clawson, T. Ramshaw, C. Lambert, M. Dixon, L. Hammill, G. Jordan. Front row: K. Greatorex, W. Ward, D. Fox, I. Lingard, J. Fennell, J. Hunt.

In their fourth Challenge Cup semi-final in five years, the Rovers again disappointed and lost 9-0 to Wakefield Trinity at Odsal on 11 April 1962. A crowd of 43,627 watched the match. *Above:* Ken Greatorex (2), awaits the challenge of Rocky Turner, watched by Len Hammill, Cliff Lambert, Gary Cooper and Terry Clawson. *Below:* Jack Fennell tries to escape the clutches of Neil Fox as reinforcements Terry Ramshaw and Len Hammill arrive.

The 1961/62 season produced Rovers' then best League record, finishing third with 57 points. They lost the Championship semi-final play-off to Wakefield 13-8. One small consolation was their participation in a tournament for the top clubs in Dublin. Wigan and Wakefield withdrew, and the competing clubs were: Featherstone, Huddersfield, Workington and Widnes. The Rovers lost their semi-final game to Widnes 35-12.

The 'A' team won the Yorkshire Senior Competition Championship in 1961/62. Several of the players, shown with coach Arthur Street (on far right), made their mark as senior players. From left to right, back row: B. Quarmby, A. Lynch, H. Brown, T. Ramshaw, L. Tonks, S. Nicholson, D. Carr, A. Morgan, J. Anderson. Front row: V. Rawes, K. Cotton, E. Broom, W.Fawley, C. Dooler, I. Lingard, B. Kennedy.

An Eastern Division Championship was introduced in 1962/63 to complement the new First Division. Hull KR claimed a unique treble in October, beating the Rovers 22-6 in the Yorkshire Cup semi-final, 29-14 in the opening First Division game, and 27-11 in the Eastern Division semi-finals – all at Craven Park. This picture shows the Rovers team in the league game, from left to right, back row: C. Clifft, V. Rawes, A. Lynch, D. Lamming, N. Hockley, E. Broom, L. Hammill. Front row: I. Lingard, C. Dooler, J. Mullaney, J. Fennell, K. Greatorex, W. Ward.

Two of Rovers' most prolific points scorers in action as Don Fox (with ball) is watched by forward Terry Clawson. Signed in 1957, Clawson gained county and international honours. In 191 senior appearances, he amassed a total of 1,091 points (487 goals and 39 tries) before his transfer to Bradford in January 1965 for £3,000.

Another famous victory over the Kangaroo touring team – 7,850 spectators watched the Rovers win 23-17 on 2 October 1963. This page shows the Rovers tries scored by Terry Ramshaw (above) and Don Fox (below). Second row forward Ramshaw was an outstanding talent, who transferred to Halifax in December 1965 for a then record fee of £5,000.

The programme for the Australia game and Rovers and Australian officials after the match. The photograph includes Aussie legends Reg Gasnier (next to Don Fox on the left) and Johnny Raper (third from right), with Gary Cooper (outside right).

OFFICIAL SOUVENIR PROGRAMME :
PRICE SIXPENCE

WEDNESDAY 2nd OCTOBER 1963

# FEATHERSTONE ROVERS
VERSUS
# Australia

Two disappointing Yorkshire Cup finals in which the Rovers were well below par, losing to Halifax 10-0 and to Hull KR 25-12.

Abe Terry in action in the 1963 Yorkshire Cup final. He was transferred from Leeds for £3,000 in December 1962 and left for Castleford in 1964, after 51 appearances. Don Fox and Harry Brown are the other Rovers players, wearing an unfamiliar white strip.

# FEATHERSTONE ROVERS R.L.F.C.

# *"Side by Side"*

### An Outline of the Careers of
### DON FOX and JOE MULLANEY
### by
### R. BAILEY

*All proceeds from the sale of this Handbook are for the*
*D. Fox / J. Mullaney Testimonial Fund*

### PRICE  -  ONE SHILLING

Two of the greatest-ever Rovers players were undoubtedly Don Fox and Joe Mullaney, both from Sharlston, who both first appeared in Rovers colours in the Coronation Cup game against Wakefield in June 1953. Their half-back partnership was established in 1953/54 and they remained in tandem until 1962. They were granted a joint testimonial in 1963, when George Potts, a local sports editor, described the combination thus 'Fox, with his forward-like frame, still has a remarkable instinct for being there and doing the right thing. Five yards from the line there is still no more dangerous scrum half in the game. Mullaney's skill, by contrast, was rapier-like, with an exciting change of pace in attack, and a split-second timing in defence which no contemporaries could better.' Both players gained county and international honours and both captained the Rovers at various stages. During his later years, Joe's career was affected by injury and he retired in 1965, with a career record of 319 appearances, 7 goals and 85 tries (a total of 269 points). Don made a successful switch to loose forward in 1963 and dominated the Rovers points scoring, breaking each record in turn. He was transferred to Wakefield in 1965. In 369 appearances he scored 162 tries and 503 goals (a total of 1,492 points). His try total remains a club record to this day.

The Mackeson Rugby League awards ran for two years in the mid-1960s, and were given to the team with the best points average in five periods during each season. Rovers won the third period, from 23 November 1964 to 9 January 1965, with a points average of 17.0. The team all received specially inscribed tankards.

Not Jack Fennell's favourite photograph, but there were many happier moments for this extremely versatile player who notched up 1,000 points (455 goals and 30 tries) in a senior career which lasted from 1952 to 1965. Fennell was another talented Rovers player who deserved, but never gained, representative honours.

Willis Fawley, Rovers' hooker, in action against Workington. He made his senior debut on 10 March 1951 and played his last game on 5 April 1967, to create a then club long-service record. Fawley scored 59 tries in 372 appearances.

At the start of a historic Challenge Cup campaign in 1967, Rovers beat Wakefield 11-7 in front of 12,500 at Featherstone. In this photograph, Ken Greatorex has scored the vital try, much to the consternation of former Rovers Don Fox and Don Metcalfe (on ground).

## CUP THRILLS

Pictures from the Featherstone-Castleford cup clash at Post Office Road on Saturday show:—

Above—The strength of the Featherstone cover as substitute Dicky Brown tries his hand. Left to right for Rovers are Wrigglesworth, Thompson, Smith and Thomas.

Left — The strength of Arnold Morgan, checked by Hardisty and Taylor, with Howe underneath and Harris behind.

Below — The try that was, but wasn't. Taylor, collared by Hartley, with Edwards sprawling and Willett coming up, was denied a score because he failed to ground properly. Cotton (left) and Jordan are the Featherstone men.

The third-round thrills against Castleford in 1967 were captured in this *Pontefract & Castleford Express* presentation. Rovers won the encounter 8-7 before 14,859 spectators. With three minutes remaining Rovers were leading 8-4, when Alan Hardisty, the Castleford stand-off, raced through from halfway to score a try. Gary Jordan, the Rovers centre, had the presence of mind to chase and force Hardisty away from the posts towards the touchline. With the score at 8-7, the result depended upon Willett's conversion. In a troublesome gale, he failed, and Rovers were through.

"Express" photographer Alf Harrison snapped both Featherstone tries at Fartown. Dooler (above) shows just how easily he found his blind-side route to the line, for the only man on his right, off the picture, was Rovers' winger Jordan.

Morgan's effort (below) shows how he beat four defenders for his finger-tip touchdown.

At last – after five Challenge Cup semi-final defeats between 1955 and 1962, the Rovers reached Wembley with a 16-8 win over Leeds at Huddersfield on 1 April 1967. A crowd of 19,217 witnessed the game.

THE RUGBY LEAGUE
CHALLENGE CUP COMPETITION

**FINAL**

**Barrow**

versus

**Featherstone
Rovers**

SATURDAY MAY 13th 1967
Kick - off 3 p.m.

**WEMBLEY**
EMPIRE STADIUM

OFFICIAL PROGRAMME · · · · · ONE SHILLING

The Rovers prepared for their Wembley date by staying at the Crystal Palace National Recreation Centre, being the first Rugby League club to do so. Its facilities were superb and the team returned to the Centre on the day after the match to show the trophy to the staff.

John Jepson, Rovers chairman, achieves his ambition to lead the team out at Wembley.

Malcolm Dixon, Rovers skipper, introduces the team to HRH The Duke of Edinburgh.

Rovers' determination shows as Smales, Cotton and Greatorex deal with Barrow winger Burgess.

Magic moments as Arnie Morgan scores Rovers' opening try (above) and Tommy Smales seals the victory with his try (below).

*Above:* Malcolm Dixon receives the trophy from Her Majesty the Queen. *Below:* The Challenge Cup-winning squad, from left to right, back row: G. Harris, J. Thompson, M. Kosanovic, A. Morgan, L. Tonks, T. Smales, D. Hartley, B. Wrigglesworth. Front row: L. Gant (coach), V. Thomas, K. Greatorex, M. Dixon, C. Dooler, M. Smith, K. Cotton, G. Jordan.

Post-match celebrations in London, with Miss Photo-Cine 1967, Cheryl Driscoll (above), and in Featherstone as the Challenge Cup comes home (below).

*The Pontefract & Castleford Express* presented this montage celebrating the great day to the club.

Supreme goal-kickers Tommy Smales (above left) and Cyril Kellett (above right), were both locals, but joined the Rovers late in their careers from other clubs. Tommy Smales was acquired from Barrow in September 1966, and in 45 consecutive games he scored 154 goals and 12 tries (including the fastest century of points in just nine games). He played his last game in October 1969, with a final total of 268 goals and 24 tries (608 points) from only 130 appearances. He had a brief spell as coach in 1974. Cyril Kellett was transferred from Hull KR in February 1968 and played until 1974. In 171 games, he kicked 557 goals and scored 15 tries (a total of 1,159 points). This tally included a record 8 goals from 8 attempts at Wembley in the 1973 Challenge Cup win over Bradford Northern.

'They fly through the air with the greatest of ease' ... to score tries. Ken Greatorex (above) scored 101 tries in 288 appearances before retiring in 1968. Carl Dooler (below) had 62 in 198 appearances before his transfer to Hull KR in 1968, having won the Lance Todd Trophy in the 1967 Wembley win.

No man deserved the title of 'Mr Featherstone Rovers' more than John Jepson, who was elected to the committee in 1946. He worked tirelessly for the club and was elected chairman in 1959, a position he held until 1976. During that period, he had the honour to lead his beloved Rovers out at Wembley in 1967, 1973 and 1974. He was also the club representative on the Rugby League Council, and in 1968/69 served that body as chairman. In 1976, he was appointed president of Rovers, a position he held until his death in 1978. John was supported throughout by his wife, Annie, who was active on the ladies committee for many years. They donated the John Jepson Trophy for the annual Player of the Season award.

## Chapter Six

# The 1970s

Upon reflection, it seems that almost everything happened to the Rovers in the 1970s, which perhaps should indicate that this decade was the most significant in the club's history. Certainly, it could be said that the team reached its zenith between 1972 and 1977. Yet, ironically, this was in a period of change. Laurie Gant, who had inspired such heights in the 1960s, resigned as coach in 1971, but within two years his successor, Peter Fox, had moulded another Challenge Cup-winning side. The Rovers excelled in their 1973 win and also registered their highest League position (second) in the one-league system – which had existed since 1905, and which the Rugby League Council subsequently decided to replace with a two-division structure.

Although there were more changes of coach, the team focused on the First Division, moving from fourth in 1975 to second in 1976, finally reaching the pinnacle in 1977. This was a record of consistency from an outstanding group of players, but a change in playing fortunes occurred rapidly. Key players in the successful pack were transferred and, two years later, the club was relegated to the Second Division. There was a strike by the Rovers players at the end of 1977/78, when the final league game at Bradford had to be cancelled and the club was fined £3,000. Further changes occurred off the field when the club's committee structure of thirteen guarantors and six elected members, which had existed since the 1930s, was reduced to form a new regime of seven members.

|  | P | W | D | L | Pts For | Agst | Pts | Posn |
|---|---|---|---|---|---|---|---|---|
| 1969/70 | 34 | 22 | 1 | 11 | 558 | 385 | 45 | 8(30) |
| 1970/71 | 34 | 14 | 1 | 19 | 572 | 635 | 29 | 20(30) |
| 1971/72 | 34 | 23 | 1 | 10 | 632 | 372 | 47 | 7(30) |
| 1972/73 | 34 | 27 | 0 | 7 | 768 | 436 | 54 | 2(30) |
| 1973/74 | 30 | 14 | 2 | 14 | 443 | 397 | 30 | 8(16) |
| 1974/75 | 30 | 19 | 1 | 10 | 431 | 339 | 39 | 4(16) |
| 1975/76 | 30 | 21 | 2 | 7 | 526 | 348 | 44 | 2(16) |
| 1976/77 | 30 | 21 | 2 | 7 | 568 | 334 | 44 | 1(16) |
| 1977/78 | 29 | 15 | 2 | 12 | 443 | 452 | 32 | 7(16) |
| 1978/79 | 30 | 8 | 1 | 21 | 501 | 549 | 17 | 14(16) |

(There were two divisions from 1973/74, Rovers playing in the First Division.)

A young Steve Nash receives his Player of the Year award. He graced the game at club, county and international level, making 201 appearances for Rovers before his then world record transfer to Salford for £15,000 in July 1975. He won the Lance Todd Trophy in the 1973 Wembley Cup Final.

The Rovers team that lost 7-4 away to Swinton on 10 January 1970. From left to right, back row: C. Kellett, A. Rhodes, J. Newlove, D. Morgan, S. Lyons, J. Thompson, D. Hartley. Front row: K. Cotton, M. Smith, J. Hay, M. Dixon, S. Nash, D. Kellett.

Back on the Challenge Cup trail and Jimmy Thompson is hidden as he scores in the satisfying 17-3 Challenge Cup semi-final win over local rivals Castleford in 1973. John Newlove (4), Steve Nash (7), Mick Smith (3) and Les Tonks celebrate. Tonks, Thompson and Smith were the only players who were members of all three Cup final teams in 1967, 1973 and 1974.

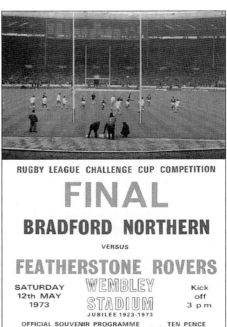

RUGBY LEAGUE CHALLENGE CUP COMPETITION

# FINAL

## BRADFORD NORTHERN

VERSUS

## FEATHERSTONE ROVERS

SATURDAY
12th MAY
1973

WEMBLEY
STADIUM
JUBILEE 1923-1973

Kick
off
3 p.m.

OFFICIAL SOUVENIR PROGRAMME          TEN PENCE

The Rovers romped to a 33-14 win over Bradford Northern in 1973, Wembley's jubilee year. The attendance for the game was 72,395, and the receipts of £125,826 constituted a world record for a rugby league game at the time. Cyril Kellett's immaculate 8 goals from 8 attempts remains a Wembley record.

Rovers electrified Wembley with 17 points in the first 20 minutes. It was the most free-scoring final in the history of the competition until Wigan's 28-24 win over Hull in 1985. *Above:* Vince Farrar scores one of Rovers' five tries. *Below:* Skipper John Newlove and his team display the Challenge Cup.

Once again, the *Pontefract & Castleford Express* was delighted to present a memento of a splendid final.

There was a quick return to Wembley for the 1974 Challenge Cup final, which was an ill-tempered game. Rovers were leading 9-8 at half time, but Warrington, orchestrated by Alex Murphy, commanded the second half and won 24-9. The final was watched by 77,400 spectators. Warrington also defeated the Rovers 4-0 in the Captain Morgan Trophy final held later in the year. This competition was limited to County Cup first round winners and only lasted one year.

Mick Smith is a lone figure in the final as a mass of Warrington players move in. Mick still shares the club record for most tries in a match – 6 against Doncaster in 1968. He scored 115 tries in 373 appearance from 1964 to 1976. He and Harry Brown were signings from the Rossington club. Harry Brown, with his bustling second-row style, made a spectacular debut, scoring a pair of tries in the 1963 Yorkshire Cup game with Leeds, but injury forced his departure after only 22 appearances.

Hopes of a third successive victory over the touring Australians, to follow the triumphs of 1959 and 1963, were thwarted in this 1973 Cup Holders *v.* Tourists clash. The Aussies won 18-13 in front of 5,059 spectators.

**THE CUP-HOLDERS**

versus

**THE TOURISTS !**

# FEATHERSTONE ROVERS

versus

# AUSTRALIA

SUNDAY 18th NOVEMBER 1973

SOUVENIR PROGRAMME

**10p**

Mal Dixon played his last game in February 1975, having scored 47 tries and 41 goals in 321 appearances. He was one of an incredibly talented trio of players signed from the junior side in 1957 – Terry Clawson and Roy Bell being the others. Mal served the club with distinction and is now chairman of the Past Players Association.

The fitness of the players was in the hands of two members from one family between 1921 and 1993. Bill Williams (above left) played for the junior team from 1913 to 1921, sharing in the remarkable success of the 1919 to 1921 side. After the Rovers made their senior debut in 1921, he played two games, but then decided to concentrate on his role as trainer to the team and carried on using his skills as a chartered physiotherapist, also coaching at various stages until 1962, when he officially retired. In the interim, his son Jim (above right), had taken up the same profession and, indeed, assisted his father with the players from the 1950s. It was natural, therefore, that Jim should succeed his father officially at the club – unofficially it was then the turn of Bill Williams to be the assistant as he found it hard to keep away and was still assisting in 1978, when he completed an incredible sixty-five-year connection with the club. Jim retired from his main employment as department head at Pontefract General Infirmary in 1984, and decided to relinquish his Rovers involvement at the same time. However, he answered the call to return from 1987 to 1993. The club was indeed fortunate to have such dedicated service from two exceptional people.

Peter Fox played 34 games for the Rovers in the mid-1950s, but, unlike his brothers Neil and Don, gained fame more as a coach than player. He had two spells coaching the Rovers from 1972 to 1975 and again from 1987 to 1991, making him the longest serving post-war coach.

THE ESSO YORKSHIRE CUP FINAL

**CASTLEFORD v FEATHERSTONE R.**

Saturday, 15th October 1977 Programme

at Headingley Ground, Leeds Price 15 pence

SPONSORED BY ESSO PETROLEUM

Rovers' dismal record in Yorkshire Cup finals continued in 1976 with a 16-12 defeat by Leeds and again in 1977 when Castleford won 17-7. The competition was discontinued after the 1992/93 season and, following another unsuccessful attempt against Bradford in 1989, the club's final record was only two wins (1940 and 1959) in ten appearances.

**1976-77**

## FIRST DIVISION

| | | P | W | D | L | F | A | Pts |
|---|---|---|---|---|---|---|---|---|
| 1 | Featherstone R. | 30 | 21 | 2 | 7 | 568 | 334 | 44 |
| 2 | St. Helens | 30 | 19 | 1 | 10 | 547 | 345 | 39 |
| 3 | Castleford | 30 | 19 | 1 | 10 | 519 | 350 | 39 |
| 4 | Hull K.R. | 30 | 18 | 1 | 11 | 496 | 415 | 37 |
| 5 | Warrington | 30 | 18 | 0 | 12 | 532 | 406 | 36 |
| 6 | Salford | *29 | 17 | 1 | 11 | 560 | 402 | 35 |
| 7 | Wigan | 30 | 15 | 2 | 13 | 463 | 416 | 32 |
| 8 | Bradford N. | 30 | 15 | 2 | 13 | 488 | 470 | 32 |
| 9 | Leeds | •29 | 14 | 2 | 13 | 467 | 439 | 30 |
| 10 | Widnes | 30 | 15 | 0 | 15 | 403 | 393 | 30 |
| 11 | Wakefield T. | 30 | 13 | 2 | 15 | 487 | 480 | 28 |
| 12 | Workington T. | 30 | 13 | 1 | 16 | 352 | 403 | 27 |
| 13 | Rochdale H. | 30 | 11 | 0 | 19 | 367 | 449 | 22 |
| 14 | Leigh | 30 | 8 | 1 | 21 | 314 | 634 | 17 |
| 15 | Barrow | 30 | 8 | 0 | 22 | 345 | 628 | 16 |
| 16 | Oldham | 30 | 7 | 0 | 23 | 322 | 666 | 14 |

*The Salford v. Leeds match was abandoned after a fatal injury to Chris Sanderson (Leeds) and not replayed. Leeds were winning 5-2 after 38 mins. but the match was declared null and void.

Rovers' first and thus far only pole position in top flight, after narrowly missing out in 1975/76, when they finished second to Salford.

The Championship side, skippered by Vince Farrar, make a special presentation to Bill Williams for his sixty-five-year association with the club. From left to right: P. Coventry, J. Thompson, R. Stone, H. Box, M. Gibbins, J. Marsden, D. Fennell (hidden), S. Evans, S. Quinn, P. Smith, V. Farrar, K. Bell, M. Mason.

Only two years after the dizzy heights of finishing as First Division Champions, Rovers were relegated to the Second Division at the end of the 1978/79 season, mainly due to the departure of stalwarts Jimmy Thompson (in action above, who had made 284 appearances for Featherstone), Vince Farrar (308), Keith Bridges (235) and Richard Stone (shown below, 261 appearances).

There were more departures at the end of the 1970s as John Newlove transferred to Hull and Harold Box to Wakefield Trinity. *Above:* John Newlove in action against Leeds in the 14-9 Challenge Cup semi-final defeat in April 1978. By the time he left Rovers, he had made 381 appearances and scored 147 tries. *Below:* Harold Box, who amassed 1,123 points (476 goals and 57 tries) in 288 appearances for Featherstone, in action against Wigan.

# Chapter Seven

# The 1980s

The outstanding feat of the 1980s was the pulsating Challenge Cup win of 1983, in which the Rovers once again excelled themselves to lift the coveted trophy for the third time in their history. Many of Rovers' famous cup victories in the past have been against the odds, but this was an exceptional win. It provided some compensation for indifferent League form. Whilst there was relief that the team was able to bounce back from the Second Division at the beginning of the decade, their position in the First Division was never secure. Rovers were relegated again in 1987, but once more were able to pull themselves back after only one year.

Variable performances affected attendances, and the situation was not helped by the Miners' Strike in the mid-1980s. With finances again a problem, the club was dealt a double blow within the space of nine months when both the Social Club and then the Main Stand were destroyed through fire. The spirit which has always been part of the Rovers' set-up again prevailed, however, and by the end of the decade the adverse situation had been reversed. A new stand and clubhouse had risen from the ashes and the ground had been sold to Wakefield Metropolitan District Council and leased back to the club. At least this ensured that Rovers were relieved of the extra heavy overheads emanating from new legislation relating to the safety of sports grounds. The introduction of the Freedom of Contract Scheme for players would, however, have strong implications for the club...

|          | P  | W  | D | L  | Pts For | Agst | Pts | Posn   |
|----------|----|----|---|----|---------|------|-----|--------|
| 1979/80* | 26 | 21 | 2 | 3  | 724     | 280  | 44  | 1(14)  |
| 1980/81  | 30 | 12 | 0 | 18 | 467     | 446  | 24  | 12(16) |
| 1981/82  | 30 | 12 | 1 | 17 | 482     | 493  | 25  | 10(16) |
| 1982/83  | 30 | 10 | 4 | 16 | 350     | 447  | 24  | 12(16) |
| 1983/84  | 30 | 11 | 2 | 17 | 464     | 562  | 24  | 12(16) |
| 1984/85  | 30 | 15 | 0 | 15 | 461     | 475  | 30  | 9(16)  |
| 1985/86  | 30 | 9  | 3 | 18 | 419     | 616  | 21  | 13(16) |
| 1986/87  | 30 | 8  | 1 | 21 | 498     | 776  | 17  | 14(16) |
| 1987/88* | 28 | 21 | 2 | 5  | 712     | 353  | 44  | 2(20)  |
| 1988/89  | 26 | 13 | 1 | 12 | 482     | 545  | 27  | 6(14)  |

* denotes Second Division.

Rovers bounced back into the First Division in 1980, using a nucleus of players from this team that faced Workington in August. From left to right, back row: K. Anderson, G. Siddall, D. Hobbs, S. Hankins, R. Handscombe, J. Gilbert, S. Evans, P. Coventry, P. Smith. Front row: G. Robinson, T. Hudson, K. Kellett, M. Morgan, J. Marsden, S. Quinn.

In 1982, the Rovers made history as the first professional side not to play in the first round of Challenge Cup. A preliminary round had been introduced and Rovers lost to Hull KR. Steve Evans, in action above against Fulham's Hussain M'Barki, played in that game but was then transferred to Hull for £70,000 before the Challenge Cup register closed. As such, he was then able to play for Hull and won a winners' medal that year. The rules were later changed to prevent this happening again.

Unexpectedly, there was instant revenge in the 1983 Challenge Cup. John Gilbert (with the ball, above) scored two tries in Rovers' classic win 11-10 win at St Helens in the third round. Bradford were beaten 11-6 in the semi-final, after which Ken Kellett (below) was chaired by supporters. Gilbert scored 81 tries in 240 appearances and Ken Kellett, who retired after the Cup final, 124 tries in 358 appearances.

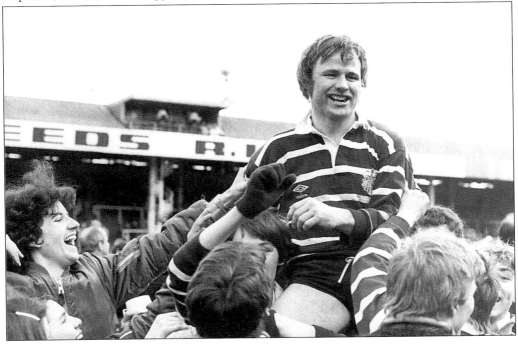

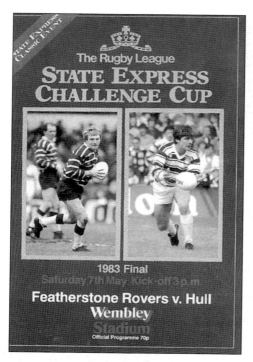

The Rugby League
**STATE EXPRESS
CHALLENGE CUP**

1983 Final
Saturday 7th May Kick-off 3 p.m.

**Featherstone Rovers v. Hull
Wembley**
Stadium
Official Programme 70p

As League Champions and Challenge Cup holders, Hull were the outstanding 4/1 favourites for this final, which made the Rovers' 14-12 win so laudable. Once again, the fighting spirit and determination which had inspired so many cup victories in the past was evident, with full credit going to coaches Alan Agar and Keith Goulding.

Chairman Bob Ashby with chief guest Lord Gormley at the pre-match team presentation.

*Above:* David Hobbs scores the first of his two tries, despite former Rover Keith Bridges' tackle.
*Below:* Tim Slatter's progress with the ball is watched anxiously by props Mick Gibbins and Steve Hankins and skipper Terry Hudson. Hobbs won the Lance Todd Trophy.

Another montage from the *Pontefract & Castleford Express*, which now hangs proudly in the club boardroom. Steve Quinn hoists the Challenge Cup and is also shown in the process of kicking his last-minute penalty goal which secured the trophy.

The 1983 Challenge Cup squad. From left to right, back row: T. Slatter, G. Siddall, M. Gibbins, D. Hobbs, N. Barker, K. Bell. Middle row: K. Goulding, N. Pickerill, R. Marsh, P. Lyman, S. Hankins, P. Johnson, K. Kellett, A. Agar. Front row: A. Banks, J. Gilbert, P. Smith, R. Ashby, T. Hudson, R. Handscombe, S. Quinn. The Wembley attendance was 84,745, which was the largest crowd the Rovers had played in front of in any of their four post-war Cup finals. Their share of the receipts of £660,000 helped to ease the financial situation, which was again causing concern.

The first floodlights were switched on against Wakefield in October 1983. In February 1985, an electrical fault linked to the floodlights caused the fire which burned down the main stand. A lifeline appeal for £100,000 was launched and here club officials gratefully receive £50,000 from the former West Riding County Council.

During the construction of the new stand, it was business as usual despite temporary facilities. The new stand was opened at the beginning of 1986/87 season, at the end of which the team was again relegated to the Second Division.

Action *v.* Salford in September 1985 as Bob Spurr is tackled near the line. The Rovers players are Mick Gibbins, Alan Banks, Keith Bell, Deryck Fox and Neil Clawson – the son of former Rover Terry Clawson.

The team bounced back into the First Division as runners-up in the Second Division at the end of 1987/88. From left to right, back row: P. Smith, P. Hughes, G. Booth, J. Grayshon, A. Dakin, G.S. Price. Front row: I. Smales, T. Staniforth, C. Bibb, D. Fox, A. Banks, P. Newlove, -?-.

**Sunday
11th October
1987**

**1st Official Tour Match
FEATHERSTONE ROVERS
V
PAPUA NEW GUINEA**

**at
3.30 p.m.**

P.N.G.R.F.L.

The Rovers entertained Papua New Guinea in October 1987, but lost 22-16. The occasion was also used for the official opening of the new clubhouse and dressing rooms, as an extension to the new stand, by the Earl of Swinton.

This fulfilled the dream of Bob Ashby, who as chairman had directed the building project since 1985. He resigned as chairman in 1987 upon his appointment as chairman to the Rugby League Board of Directors, and was then made club president – an honour he still holds today. The current chairman, Richard Evans, is in the background.

Featherstone and Oldham contested an exhilarating Second Division Premiership final at Old Trafford in May 1988. Rovers trailed 22-0 after only 32 minutes, but in an amazing comeback were leading 26-22 with four minutes remaining. Oldham then scored to win 28-26. There was some consolation in Graham Steadman's try (above), but the dejection showed on the faces of the Rovers players (below).

Featherstone Rovers, 1988/89. From left to right, back row: J. Bastian, G. Siddall, K. Harrison, P. Smith, S. Quinn, I. Smales, G. Bell, P. Hughes, J. Grayshon. Front row: K. Bell, P. Newlove, P. Lyman, G. Steadman, D. Fox, A. Banks, C. Bibb, T. Clark, R. Marsh, P. Carey.

New Zealand's 44-20 win means that the Rovers have never beaten the Kiwis. The attendance of 2,773 was the smallest ever at Post Office Road against any touring side. In the Kiwi team that day was Brendon Tuuta, who was to sign for the club three years later.

Rovers achieved a then club record high score in their Yorkshire Cup first-round 86-18 win over Keighley in September 1989. Alan Banks is the player in action, with Jeff Grayshon and Chris Burton supporting. Banks was a stylish centre who scored 46 tries in 233 appearances. Chris Bibb, the Rovers full-back, equalled the club record of 6 tries in the match.

Mark Knapper kicked 13 goals in this match – establishing a record that still stands. Here he receives his man of the match award from Malcolm Reilly. Knapper only made 16 appearances before leaving in 1991.

Rovers supporters have been treated to many goal- and points-scoring heroes during the club's history, but the king of them has to be centre Steve Quinn. He joined Rovers in February 1976 from York, making his debut in the Challenge Cup tie with Wakefield. Rovers won 23-9, with Steve kicking four goals at the start of a memorable career. He signed off in his last game away against Leeds in December 1988, having kicked 1,200 goals and 10 drop goals and scored 75 tries – an astonishing total of 2,656 points – in 389 appearances. His legacy contains club records for the most goals in a season (163), sharing the fastest century of points scored (9 matches), and playing and scoring in every club game in the 1979/80 season (31 matches).

114

Another disappointing Yorkshire Cup final at Leeds on 5 November 1989, when Bradford triumphed 20-14. Peter Smith is shown scoring his consolation try.

Paul Newlove scores against Leigh in October 1989 – this was to become a familiar sight for Rovers supporters, as he topped the try-scoring list with 18 in his first season.

Keith Bell, the youngest of four brothers to play for Rovers, is the longest serving player in the club's history. He made his senior debut against Doncaster (away) in November 1971, and ended his career in 1989 when he went to Hunslet on a free transfer. In 19 seasons he made 417 appearances, scoring 58 tries, but he had a particular liking for drop goals – he landed 67, which must be a record in itself.

Another Rovers stalwart to call it a day in 1989 was Peter Smith, whose 110 career tries was a record for a forward. He made 417 appearances, and but for injury, which at one stage restricted him to only twelve matches in three seasons, would surely have broken Jim Denton's club record of 440 appearances.

# Chapter Eight

# The 1990s

It was difficult to concentrate on much else in the 1990s other than the advent of Super League and summer football. These momentous developments in the game surfaced in April 1995, when the idea of a launch in 1996 was put forward. At that time, in an attempt to rationalise existing clubs into the proposed twelve-club league, mergers were suggested with Featherstone, Castleford and Wakefield forming one Calder club. The idea was not well received (to put it mildly), and it was then said that qualification would be linked to the final First Division table of 1994/95. Rovers had finished eleventh, and were therefore hopeful of Super League status. However, it was then decided that there had to be a Super League presence in London and Europe and, as such, London Broncos and Paris St Germain were included, to the exclusion of Featherstone and Salford. It was galling, perhaps, that this attempt to establish a club in Paris soon floundered, but the decision could have a profound effect on Rovers' history. Linked with this was the move to summer rugby, something the Rovers had advocated many years previously, in the Framework for the Future document, which laid down the criteria for Super League acceptance. To accommodate this, the club became a limited company in 1997 and improved its spectator facilities.

As the players' contract system became established, with increased player power and mobility, Rovers, like most clubs, had to heed the invasion of players from Australia and New Zealand. The fashion and competition for these (often transient) players greatly increased the playing costs, especially for the smaller clubs like Featherstone. Although some proved popular and good value, such as Brendon Tuuta, such short-term contracts and mobility did not help to construct a constant and stable player base. The Rovers were Second Division Champions in 1992/93, scoring a record number of points in a league campaign (996), with three players setting up new records for tries and points scored. The fixture list in that season comprised of eight clubs in the Second Division, each playing the other four times. The establishment of any record is worthy of celebration, but needs to be placed in context. Since then, in their post-Super League First Division experience, they have maintained a position within the top five, but only reached the Grand Final in 1998.

The club's achievements in the Challenge Cup were never matched in the Regal Trophy competition, which was introduced in 1971 (originally as the John Player Cup) and continued until 1996. In its twenty-five year history, the best the Rovers could achieve was to reach the third round, which they managed on only four occasions.

|  | P | W | D | L | Pts For | Agst | Pts | Posn |
|---|---|---|---|---|---|---|---|---|
| 1989/90 | 26 | 10 | 0 | 16 | 479 | 652 | 20 | 10(14) |
| 1990/91 | 26 | 12 | 1 | 13 | 533 | 592 | 25 | 8(14) |
| 1991/92 | 26 | 11 | 0 | 15 | 449 | 570 | 22 | 13(14) |
| 1992/93* | 28 | 24 | 1 | 3 | 996 | 352 | 49 | 1(8) |
| 1993/94 | 30 | 13 | 1 | 16 | 651 | 681 | 27 | 11(16) |
| 1994/95 | 30 | 10 | 1 | 19 | 613 | 775 | 21 | 11(16) |
| 1995+ | 20 | 11 | 0 | 9 | 420 | 431 | 22 | 5(11) |
| 1996 | 20 | 12 | 2 | 6 | 557 | 371 | 26 | 4(11) |
| 1997 | 20 | 8 | 1 | 11 | 408 | 395 | 17 | 7(11) |
| 1998 | 30 | 17 | 1 | 12 | 779 | 613 | 33 | 4(11) |
| 1999 | 28 | 19 | 1 | 8 | 714 | 466 | 39 | 5(18) |
| 2000 | 28 | 20 | 1 | 7 | 795 | 523 | 41 | 5(18) |
| 2001 | 28 | 17 | 2 | 9 | 825 | 401 | 36 | 5(19) |

\* denotes Second Division. + denotes advent of Super League and First Division.

Powerful winger Owen Simpson, transferred from Keighley in 1990, formed a formidable partnership with Paul Newlove. In three seasons, before Newlove's departure to Bradford, they scored 155 tries (Newlove 86, Simpson 69). Simpson's final total before he retired in 1996 was 85 tries from 125 appearances. Carl Gibson is the other Rovers player in the picture.

Ikram Butt, shown in action against Sheffield, scored 67 tries in 168 appearances from 1990 to 1995. He became the first man of Asian descent to play for England in 1995 and was transferred to London Broncos later that year.

Two Featherstone favourites, with Deryck Fox on the shoulder of Jeff Grayshon. Jeff was signed from Bradford in 1988 at the age of thirty-nine to add experience to the Rovers pack. He made 100 appearances before leaving in 1991, and ended his playing days at Batley, a remarkable fitness achievement. Whilst at Featherstone, he played in the front row opposite his son, Paul (propping for Bradford), and became a grandfather. Deryck Fox had two spells with the club, the first lasting from 1983 to 1992, when he was transferred to Bradford Northern for £140,000. He maintained the tradition of famous scrum-halves from Featherstone. He returned in 1995, and when he retired in 1998, his total Rovers career record was 78 tries, 328 goals and 52 drop goals – a total of 1,020 points – in 308 appearances.

As Second Division champions in 1992/93, the team display the trophy at Post Office Road with coach Steve Martin.

In the Divisional Premiership, Rovers reached the final with a 35-12 win over Dewsbury. Ian Smales is pictured scoring one of the tries, which gave him a club record of most tries in a season by a forward (22).

In the Premiership final at Old Trafford on 16 May 1993, Francis Maloney heads to score one of the tries in the 20-16 win over Workington.

More celebrations after the Premiership final victory. Paul Newlove won the man of the match award, and set up a new club record of most tries in a season (48). Within weeks of this occasion, he had transferred to Bradford Northern for a record £250,000.

Action from a game against Halifax, as Gary H. Price attempts to break out of defence, watched by Brendon Tuuta and Leo Casey (right). Tuuta signed from Western Suburbs in 1990. He was a firm favourite with his no-nonsense style and, after transferring to Castleford in 1995, returned for one more season in 1999.

This is how the *Pontefract & Castleford Express* saw the Antipodean influence in the 1990s.

Andy Currier was signed from Widnes in 1993 for £150,000, but a pre-season practice match injury ruled him out for the whole campaign. He returned in 1994, scoring two tries on his debut against Wigan (shown here), but was later transferred to Warrington in 1995, after making only 11 appearances for Rovers.

Mark Aston scoring against St Helens in 1995. Mark cost £100,000 from Sheffield in 1994. He returned to Sheffield in 1996, having made 35 appearances for Rovers.

Featherstone Rovers, 1994/95. From left to right, back row: J. Smith, G. Lingard, E. Rombo, S. Tuffs, J. Nadioli, M. Calland, C. Gibson. Middle row: D. Evans, L. Casey, F. Banquet, O. Simpson, M. Pearson, N. Roebuck. Front row: M. Aston, C. Bibb, G. Southernwood, S. Molloy, R. Gunn, A. Miller, A. Thompson. The 1995/96 season was shortened to prepare for the switch to Super League and summer football in 1996.

Martin Pearson holds two club records – most points in a match (40 from 4 tries and 12 goals in the 60-10 home defeat of Whitehaven in November 1995) and most points in a season (391 in 1992/93, with 28 tries, 139 goals and 1 drop goal). Also in this picture is Chris Bibb, who shares the record of 6 tries in a match, a tally he obtained in the Yorkshire Cup game with Keighley in September 1989.

Roy Powell, pictured in action (with the ball) against Whitehaven. Roy joined the club from Bradford in 1995 and was a popular and inspirational figure. He departed in 1998 to coach at Rochdale and the rugby league world was shocked by his untimely death later that year. His memory is preserved in the man of the match award in the recently revived Yorkshire v. Lancashire game.

Hopes of more Wembley glory evaporated in the Challenge Cup semi-final in April 1995. Mark Aston is shown kicking a late goal to take the Elland Road scoreboard to a final tally of 39-22, after a game in which Rovers never recovered from a 2nd minute interception try by Gary Schofield.

The 1998 First Division Grand Final between Wakefield Trinity and Featherstone was praised as a 'night to remember' after a classic encounter. Rovers were leading 22-18 late in the second half when they had a try by Karl Pratt controversially disallowed. This would have sealed the game in their favour, but in the final minutes Stephenson scored for Trinity to give them a famous 24-22 victory.

Karl Pratt, Rovers' talented winger, was transferred to Leeds after the Grand Final for £70,000, having scored 30 tries in 48 appearances. Such transfer fees, the salvation of Rovers so many times in the past, will diminish in the future as a consequence of the changing contractual climate and the greater polarisation of the game.

A necessary sign of the times: the RJB Mining chairman, Mr R. Budge, signs the sponsorship deal with Rovers official Steve Wagner – which, together with a grant from the Sports Ground Initiative Trust, helped to provide the RJB Family Stand. Officially opened on Good Friday 1997, it has 1,600 seats and raised the ground capacity to 6,800. In the deal, the ground became the Lionheart Stadium and the club also took the opportunity to introduce its pirate logo.

An aerial view of one of the most compact stadiums in the Northern Ford Premiership.

In the last match of their 2001 league programme, the Rovers amassed their highest-ever score – 92-2 against York, with 17 tries and 12 goals. Here, Neil Lowe registers his contribution.

The immediate future of Rovers rests with, from left to right, back row: J. Stokes, S. Dooler, R. Hellwell, G. Morgan, D. Evans, G. Lord. Middle row: P. Roe (manager), R. Chapman, N. Lowe, S. Dickens, D. Seal, C. Booth, L. Williamson, P. Darley, I. Fairhurst (assistant manager). Front row: M. Bramald, S. Jackson, A. Bastow, J. Rooney, M. Rhodes, G. Swinson, C. Spurr. Danny Evans is continuing a family tradition. His grandfather, Ray Evans, and his father, Barry, also played for the Rovers. Skipper Jamie Rooney, who is carrying on the tradition of point-scoring scrum-halves, has to date registered 812 points (38 tries, 316 goals, 28 drop goals) in 82 appearances.